New Horizons 10/13 £12.99

Middlesbrough College
Learning Resources Centre

MIDDLESBROUGH COLLEGE
LEARNING RESOURCES CLASSROOM
WITHDRAWN

Class No 658.872 Wil
Accession 096586
Location L

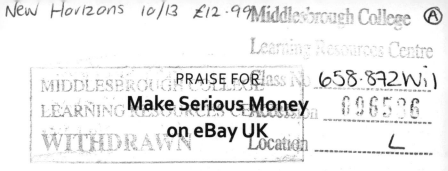

PRAISE FOR
Make Serious Money on eBay UK

"To sell successfully on eBay, you have to create a picture of yourself as a seller that will make buyers trust you and place big bids. In *Make Serious Money on eBay UK* expert Dan Wilson explains how to stand out from the crowd."
Daily Telegraph

"Written with wit, insight and a wealth of experience."
Manager

"Fancy becoming a millionaire without leaving home? ... It is possible to make extra cash by selling almost anything and, with a worldwide market and low overheads, a third of all new businesses are now set up on the net. If you want to get in on the action ... *Make Serious Money on eBay UK* by Dan Wilson tells you how."
The Sun

"Some of the tricks of trading on eBay... revealed for the first time by an insider. His advice is timely."
Sunday Mirror

"Get in on the craze that's sweeping the technological world with this guide. Learn how to dig up the best bargains and how to market your own treasures, all while keeping your personal details secure."
Good Book Guide

10656143

00096586

Middlesbrough College

Learning Resources Centre

Class No 658·872 Wil

Accession 096586

Location ____L____

Make Serious Money
on
eBay UK,
Amazon and Beyond

Dan Wilson

MIDDLESBROUGH COLLEGE
LEARNING RESOURCES CENTRE
WITHDRAWN

Learning Resources Centre
Middlesbrough College
Dock Street
Middlesbrough
TS2 1AD

NICHOLAS BREALEY
PUBLISHING

London • Boston

This revised third edition first published by
Nicholas Brealey Publishing in 2013

3–5 Spafield Street
Clerkenwell, London
EC1R 4QB, UK
Tel: +44 (0)20 7239 0360
Fax: +44 (0)20 7239 0370

20 Park Plaza
Boston
MA 02116, USA
Tel: (888) BREALEY
Fax: (617) 523 3708

www.nicholasbrealey.com
www.wilsondan.co.uk

First edition published in 2007
Second edition published in 2009, revised in 2011
© Dan Wilson 2007, 2009, 2011, 2013
First published as *Make Money on eBay UK* in 2005

The right of Dan Wilson to be identified as the author of this
work has been asserted in accordance with the Copyright,
Designs and Patents Act 1988.

ISBN: 978-1-85788-608-5
eISBN: 978-1-85788-958-1

The screen illustrations have been reproduced with the
permission of eBay Inc. COPYRIGHT © EBAY INC.
ALL RIGHTS RESERVED.

This book is not endorsed by eBay (UK) Ltd. The views and
opinions expressed are those of the author.

British Library Cataloguing in Publication Data
A catalogue record for this book is available from the
British Library.

All rights reserved. No part of this publication may be
reproduced, stored in a retrieval system, or transmitted, in any
form or by any means, electronic, mechanical, photocopying,
recording and/or otherwise without the prior written
permission of the publishers. This book may not be lent, resold,
hired out or otherwise disposed of by way of trade in any form,
binding or cover other than that in which it is published,
without the prior consent of the publishers.

Printed in the UK by Clays Ltd, St Ives plc.

Contents

Welcome to the world of eBay, Amazon and ecommerce

This is the latest incarnation of a book I first wrote back in 2004 – but don't worry, you haven't picked up an old, repackaged volume. This new edition is so up to date it's sizzling and it's completely revised and revamped. In a very real sense, it's a totally new book. The information on eBay has been entirely overhauled and pretty much half the book is entirely new. Rest assured, though, I've kept the best bits that thousands of readers over the years have found immensely useful, as well as adding lots, lots more.

One feature that I hope you'll find of particular use are the 'Inside Information' sections peppered throughout the book. These give you a real insight into certain aspects of eBay, Amazon or ecommerce and often have my personal spin on them. There are also dozens of 'Tips' – nuggets of advice that are vital to smooth your way and improve your experience.

Whichever way you approach making money online, there's no better way to learn than from what others have done. Whether they succeeded or failed, you can learn from their story. That's why the book includes a selection of case studies about people who are already trading, most of which are brand new for this edition.

There's just one thing to remember: all the screengrabs, facts, figures, web addresses and prices are current as I write. However, the web changes fast, so by the time you read this book they may well have changed too. If something has altered don't worry, as you should be able to find the latest information by searching Google.

WHY READ THIS BOOK? >

My aim in this book is to take you on a journey to making money online. I start small, by showing you how to dip your toe into the relatively gentle nursery pool of eBay. There you'll learn the basics of selling online, sourcing products that sell profitably, compiling listings that contain all the information buyers need to buy from you and much more. You'll also get the low-down on packaging and sending items, getting the best postage deals and building an efficient and profitable operation.

The business you spawn on eBay will help you tackle the mighty Amazon. While this represents a huge ecommerce and commercial opportunity, it's a daunting place to do business for the beginner, but you'll have the advantage of already having honed your skills. I explain how you can plug into Amazon, find more customers and sell ever more efficiently with multichannel software and other valuable tools and services.

Where you choose to set sail for next is up to you. You could explore other marketplaces on the web and peddle your wares there, or you could take on the choppy waters of Google and establish your own trading post by creating a webstore and promoting it with Adwords, thus being able to pocket all the takings yourself rather than shelling out chunks of your hard-earned cash on selling fees. The great joy of having your own website is that you're your own master, but with that freedom comes responsibility.

If you want to build a truly dynamic business that's firing on all cylinders, you need to be selling on every available and relevant platform. That's where this book is unique – it's the only guide available that's aimed squarely at the British entrepreneur who wants to build a multichannel online business. I give you information on alternative websites like Rakuten (sometimes called Play. com), which is developing some interesting options for SMEs, and fast-growing options such as Etsy and Notonthehighstreet. com.

What is more, I consider the international possibilities that exist for anyone who cares to have a go at trading successfully with buyers abroad. It's astonishing how few eBay and Amazon sellers actually do sell overseas when doing so represents such a massive opportunity.

This book also looks at the myriad of tools and services on the market that can help you build a better business – for your online presence, but also for your day-to-day operations. There are many different suggestions about software and widgets you can get your hands on to improve your business. I also offer tons of inside information garnered from my years working in ecommerce. I'll also suggest some more generic, but vital, skills you may want to develop, whether that's taking an interest in web marketing, becoming adept at web analytics, or getting to know about the laws that govern business and how to manage your business more efficiently.

So everything is here: Master eBay. Take on Amazon. Build a webstore. Explore the various different ways to sell. Continually seek to refine and improve your business. Become the captain of your own successful, profitable and rewarding ecommerce business. All of that and more is why you need this book.

ALL ABOUT YOU >

I will guide you on the journey from being a novice seller to becoming a confident online trader and will set you well on the way to becoming a profitable multichannel online business. Nevertheless, it's simply not possible – or even desirable – to shepherd you click by click through the entire process of selling online. To this end, I've made some assumptions about your existing skills and expertise.

You're a confident computer user

Whether you're accessing the web with a PC or a Mac, or even an iPad or a smartphone, everything in this book assumes that you're a confident and competent user of computers and the web. This doesn't mean you're Bill Gates or a total whizzkid, just that you have a reasonable feel for what you're doing with your device.

This is important for a couple of reasons. First, such is the variety of computers, web browsers and apps you might be using that it would be impossible to describe specific steps that are relevant and useful for everyone. Doing so would also be quite dull and make the book far too long. In addition, eBay, and other websites, look different depending on how you access them. As a result, I'm going to trust you to work out many of the simpler things for yourself.

The second reason is that as I've already noted, the details change. Websites move stuff around and out-of-date instructions are actually more confusing than none at all. So some of the screengrabs will be different from what you actually see, but the key is not to panic and to apply the general principles I'm sharing with you.

You've mastered online buying

My second assumption is that you've registered on eBay, made some bids and Buy it Nows, had some sort of introduction to Feedback and also managed to discover My eBay. Buying on eBay will also mean that by the time you start selling, you have some feedback points (which are vital) and a sound notion of the eBay basics. If you've identified that there's an opportunity to make money on eBay and Amazon, you may already be an accomplished online buyer – but if you're not, it's time to up your skills.

For instance, it's very important to buy as well as sell on eBay because it teaches you much about the nuances and complications of the marketplace. It's not that eBay is particularly complex, but there is a huge amount you need to know about and buying is a great way to find your eBay sea-legs. In fact, all through this book I'll be urging you to 'carry on buying', because it enables you to look through a customer's eyes and assess what's good practice and what isn't.

As you develop your ecommerce business, make sure you keep an eye on what competitors and others are doing well. I like to buy regularly from a variety of retailers and sellers, including Amazon and eBay, and I treat it as research. I like to see what companies big and small are doing to maximise the ecommerce opportunity and it's often fascinating to see what they're doing right – and wrong.

You have an adventurous spirit

Fortune favours the brave. The most important assumption I'm making about you is that you have buckets of keenness and that you're willing to roll up your sleeves, get your hands dirty and have a go. I can show you how to make your ecommerce business work, but only you can actually do it.

Someone who has never made a mistake has never made anything – and that includes money. This book is part manifesto, part handbook and part roadmap, all rolled into one.

There are no prizes for shyness or timidity and embarking on anything new is always a bit daunting. Nevertheless, the rewards are real and they can be yours if you've got zeal and enthusiasm.

AND ALL ABOUT ME >

My experience with ecommerce began in 1999 when I was part of the team that founded eBay in the UK. By then eBay had made an enormous splash in the US, although in the UK it was almost unknown and, if truth be told, was treated with a fair amount of suspicion. The internet was still an exciting but largely unexplored frontier for most people back then.

I started off recruiting sellers to the eBay marketplace and worked mainly on attracting sellers of stamps and coins to put their wares on the online bazaar. We never imagined that in the years to come the auction site would become a regular part of British life.

I stayed with eBay as it grew from obscure infancy into one of the biggest, most visited and profitable web businesses in the world. Over that time ecommerce developed, and eBay changed too. The company bought PayPal, which made paying for items at home and abroad immeasurably easier. And the arrival of Buy It Now meant that eBay wasn't just about auctions any longer.

Buyers could choose to bag a bargain then and there. In fact, BIN has proved so successful that more items sell that way on the site than via auctions these days.

Since I left eBay in 2006, I've maintained my relationship with ecommerce and I've watched as it's become about much more than simply eBay. I make a living by writing and as a digital marketing adviser and I've acted as an ecommerce consultant to businesses large and small, from giants like BT to tiny start-ups. It's small businesses that are genuinely my passion and I find helping a small business transform and grow hugely rewarding. SMEs don't have deep pockets or the ability to mount big campaigns, so you need to burst onto the ecommerce scene on a shoestring. That's why everything I suggest in this book is possible to achieve and usually inexpensive.

I'm also editor of a blog and news site called Tamebay.com and my colleague Chris and I write daily about all aspects of eBay, Amazon, ecommerce and small business. We bring you the breaking news as well as bags of advice to help you run a successful ecommerce business. In doing this I've broadened my knowledge of ecommerce, learnt tons more about how Amazon works and really immersed myself in the industry.

THE ECOMMERCE OPPORTUNITY >

It's nearly twenty years since buying online was introduced (eBay and Amazon both launched in 1995, although history doesn't record the date of the first online transaction) and more than a decade since doing so became a widespread, normal activity. And Britain leads the way when it comes to buying online – over £1000 a year, by head of population more than any other country in the world. Not even the Americans, Germans or Japanese spend more. In fact, pundits predict that 25% of all consumer spending in Britain will be online by 2015.

There are lots of reasons for this. Napoleon denigrated the English as merely 'a nation of shopkeepers', and we have a trading mentality that could well be the result of being an island people. But our commercial nous and love of a bargain are actually real advantages in the fast-paced and cut-throat world of internet retailing. The UK also has a highly developed consumer culture, internet coverage is pretty much 100%, access to credit cards and debit cards is nearly universal and there is also a strong infrastructure. It goes without saying that an effective postal service and a competitive courier market for bulkier goods are vital to the success of ecommerce.

Ecommerce comprises everything that's sold online. That includes your weekly grocery shop, which many households have been doing online for years and represents a significant chunk of the UK online spend. However, for the purposes of this book two ecommerce giants are of particular interest: eBay and Amazon.

Despite eBay's fame and familiarity, lots of people don't have a sense of how big the site actually is. To give you an idea of its scale, try to imagine a real-life market of the same size. If eBay UK were a market, it would have 16 million visitors every month. There would be 10 million items up for sale from millions of people and nearly 200,000 businesses.

Globally, eBay is even bigger. It operates in more than 40 countries and has more than 200 million members across the planet. Quite simply, it is the biggest marketplace in the world, trading billions of pounds' worth of merchandise every year. Even so, there's still room for you.

As for Amazon, it's difficult to know exactly how big it is. We know it's the biggest online retailer in the world, but the company reveals little about the extent of its own sales compared to those by sellers on the site. Amazon also doesn't provide country-by-country numbers, but what we do know is that Amazon UK is considered a serious competitor to the High Street. Businesses like HMV, Comet and small bookshops all cite Amazon as the key to their troubled times (even if they may be said to be looking for a scapegoat). Even firms that have successfully surfed the wave of growth in ecommerce, such as John Lewis and Argos, are critical of Amazon's power.

Considerations about particular websites aside, what can be said with certainty is that ecommerce is huge, it continues to grow and, moreover, it continues to grow faster than the UK economy in general. Indeed, the most heartening aspect of ecommerce over the past five years or so of global economic meltdown has been the surprising health and vigour of online sales. Even in times when the national economy has been in recession and retail spending retracting, ecommerce has expanded with double-digit growth. Each Christmas selling season has been bigger (sometimes much bigger) than the year before for more than a decade and that shows no signs of slowing.

That's why I'm optimistic and bullish about the future. In so many ways the internet is rewriting the rules of business so that truly novel opportunities have opened up – and people who might never have dreamed of a career in retail or business can take advantage.

WHO THIS BOOK IS FOR >

There are countless ways to make eBay and ecommerce work for you whatever your situation, but this book is especially designed for some specific groups.

Aspiring small traders

One activity that eBay in particular is very good for is generating a bit of income on the side. Now, that can mean different things to different people. It could be that you just want to sell on a few bits here and there to generate a modicum of extra cash; or you could be after something more substantial to supplement their main income.

Earning cash this way is particularly good for retired people – I know plenty of over-70s who find that the challenge of ecommerce keeps them sharp and they enjoy the extra money. It's also an option suited to young mums who need the flexibility of being their own boss but don't want to go back into work full time. A small eBay operation can easily fit around the kids and anyone with young children can always do with a little extra dough.

Young people and students are another group who can benefit from plugging into eBay like this. Selling this way fits brilliantly around studies and social life and bright young things will often have their finger on the pulse of new trends and emerging fashions, which means they have an advantage in understanding what sells. If I was a student now, I wouldn't be taking a bar job on minimum wage, I'd be selling on eBay.

Five-to-niners

Many people have the ambition of starting a business but find that in the current difficult climate it's not possible to quit the day job and start trading. That's why part-time entrepreneurs – those who come home and work on their new business from 5pm to 9pm – are so attracted to ecommerce.

Their ultimate aim is giving up the employment drudge and ditching the boss, but by proving the concept of the business in their spare time, they can better understand what they need to do to succeed in the future while they still enjoy the security of a salary.

Businesses going from bricks to clicks

In web industry parlance, high street shops that people visit in person to purchase goods are called (deliberately dismissively) 'bricks and mortar' shops. So it makes sense that an established retail store that develops a web presence and sells online is called a 'bricks and clicks' business.

Such organisations have already sorted out many of the necessary logistics: they have a ready supply of goods to sell and they should benefit from a well-developed eye for consumer trends. They should also know all about stock and distribution, so theoretically all they need to achieve is to translate what they do in the shop to the environment of the web. Nevertheless, that's not a smooth transition and in fact it's harder than it sounds, so even established companies will find something of interest in this book.

Ecommerce entrepreneurs

Ecommerce entrepreneurs are business opportunists. They usually have some money behind them and are hungry and impatient to put it to work generating profits. Many entrepreneurs are attracted to ecommerce because there are relatively few barriers to entry and it's possible to have an effective operation up and running from scratch in a matter of weeks.

The other facet of an ecommerce business that such people usually have is access to stock that needs to be sold. Their funds also enable them to get good deals, and better discounts, by bargaining with wholesalers and offering immediate cash payment.

What is more, the real advantage entrepreneurs have when they enter the fray of selling online is a clear mind. They're driven by an uncomplicated urge to make money and thus they tend to be unsentimental and focused on results.

One thing I've observed over the years is that some other people who've started to sell online don't have this drive. I recall one woman who said she'd always loved jewellery, so she opened an online shop selling some really nice pieces and was as happy as Larry for a year. The problem was that she wasn't really concentrating on building a business, but rather was having a lovely time playing shop, surrounded by the shiny baubles she was selling. At the end of the year, she realised that she'd hardly made a bean. That's the kind of mistake that entrepreneurs don't make.

Established growth seekers

Every day's a school day. And the final group of people I've thought a lot about as I've been writing this book are those who are already selling on eBay and Amazon and are keen to develop their business further to sell more and make more money. It's impossible to know exactly how many businesses are already selling online, but I'd be surprised if it was fewer than 250,000.

If you're already busy selling online and building your business, it's a constant challenge to keep abreast of changes and developments. Whether it's an overhaul of Royal Mail fees or a reorganisation of Amazon's categories, such changes are disruptive. You can also benefit from dozens of tools and services to help you run your business more effectively – you just need to know what they are.

So even if you've been trading online for years, there's plenty in this book that will help you and give you the inspiration to make a positive difference to your enterprise.

Without further ado, let's start benefiting from the ecommerce opportunity by taking a long, hard look at how to make the most of eBay.

Part I | Mastering eBay and building a business

When it comes to ecommerce, there's only one place to start. eBay provides a low-investment, low-risk gateway for entrepreneurs interested in getting their share of the action. It offers access to a readymade global marketplace populated by 200 million buyers, as well as off-the-peg tools to help sellers promote, manage and develop their sales.

A VERY BRIEF HISTORY OF eBAY >

On Labor Day 1995, a Silicon Valley coder called Pierre Omidyar launched what was to become eBay onto an unsuspecting internet. Originally, it was called Auctionweb and soon it was attracting a small but loyal following of geeks who used it to trade collectables and tech equipment. The site was primitive and for Pierre it was a labour of love, not a business.

As it grew, Auctionweb started to attract attention. Soon his web service provider began charging him more to account for the huge leap in web traffic the site was taking. Reluctantly, Pierre started charging a few cents for the service and soon small payments flooded in. Pierre wondered if he had stumbled onto something special.

At the heart of eBay lie two key principles. One was that the market had to be as free as was possible. Existing marketplaces (stock exchanges or the oil market, for instance) benefited bigger players and established traders. Prices and conditions were fixed to favour vested interests. It was rarely possible for outsiders to compete fairly.

He also believed that prices were better set by buyers rather than sellers. After all, what is a fair market price other than what someone is readily willing to pay? This concept was central to Pierre's affection for auctions. In an auction sellers are able to set the minimum price they are willing to accept and if someone thinks that is a fair price they will buy. If two or more people are willing to pay the price, or more, they bid against each other until the highest price they are willing to pay is established. The fair market price is set by buyers on the basis of what they think something is worth rather than by outside controls, cartels or vested interests.

The second touchstone of eBay's ethos lies with the simple maxim, codified by Pierre as the most important of the eBay values: people are basically good. He saw it in the earliest days of eBay and it still lies at the core of eBay's rules. It is manifested in the feedback system and also in the leap of faith that people have to take to trade with strangers online.

> 1995: Pierre Omidyar founds eBay in San Jose, California
> 1996: eBay introduces Feedback systems
> 1996: eBay hires first Customer Support rep, Jim Griffith
> 1998: Meg Whitman joins ebay as CEO
> 1998: The company goes public with the eBay IPO on the Nasdaq
> 1999: eBay buys alando.de, later becomes eBay Germany
> 1999: eBay.co.uk and eBay.au open for businesses
> 2001: eBay introduces Buy It Now feature
> 2001: eBay buys PayPal
> 2007: John Donohoe succeeds Whitman to become eBay CEO

eBAY TODAY IN A NUTSHELL >

eBay is now a marketplace where individuals and businesses sell to an online audience of about 15 million people a month in the UK. Global in scope, eBay helps you buy and sell too with people all over the world.

Sellers offer goods for sale using an online form to post pictures and a written description describing the goods for sale and buyers can either bid using an online auction system or buy instantly using the Buy It Now feature. Buyers judge the trustworthiness of sellers using a feedback system of user reviews. Some eBay sellers are accredited as Top-rated Sellers for delivering consistent good service and get better visibility in search and other perks.

Almost universally, buyers pay sellers using the online payments processor PayPal, which is owned by eBay. Sellers sometimes offer Free P&P to buyers, but if there are carriage costs they are typically covered by the buyer. Postage costs are detailed on the View Item particulars when the buyers examine the item.

Once payment is received by the sellers, the item is dispatched. Sellers pay listing fees to make their wares available for sale on eBay (but do look out for free listing promos!) and also pay a Final Value Fee commission on a successful sale. The listing fee and commission depend on the value of the goods sold and the category they were listed in. Both buyer and seller then leave feedback for their trading partner depending on how the trade went.

In the event of a sale going awry, buyers are covered by eBay Buyer Protection and sellers who get ripped off by a buyer (usually because of a dodgy payment) are protected too by PayPal.

Increasingly eBay is becoming an outlet for bigger retailers and high street names and is moving away from the 'hobby sellers' who were the mainstay in the past. But that said, many small businesses prosper on the site and there is still an army of individuals selling a few bits and bobs to turn a shilling.

It's the nursery for any budding ecommerce entrepreneur for three key reasons.

BUILT FOR BEGINNERS >

Other marketplaces, especially Amazon, require you to have an established commercial operation up and ready at the get-go. You need to provide them with all manner of business bona fides and details when you register. eBay isn't like that and is open to all. That means you can start selling very quickly indeed, and have your first items up for sale in minutes.

REPEATABLE SUCCESS >

If you can make it there, you'll make it anywhere. As you strive for success on eBay, you'll learn all the skills you'll need elsewhere. Crafting superb listings that convert browsers into buyers, learning the labyrinth of postal services and couriers and even dealing with tricky customers are all vital skills and entirely transferable to wherever you sell online.

Learning the ropes on eBay is also good for honing your competitive skills and helping you understand that it's a fairly cut-throat and relentless marketplace out there. eBay is very competitive and you're fighting other sellers to get the attention of the buyers. It's good practice.

ANYTHING'S FOR SALE >

The particular joy of eBay, and its unique selling point, is its flexibility. It's the only online marketplace where you can sell quite literally anything. That said, there are some exclusions that we look at later in the book, but they're mostly common sense and not particularly onerous.

And this freedom really is great news for the ecommerce beginner. You may have a solid plan and a grand scheme to sell glorious brand new widgets imported from China or free-range organic, hand-crafted artisan sprockets exclusive to you from craftspeople in Borneo. Nevertheless, diving in head first is not the finest plan.

The best way to get started on eBay is with a good old-fashioned clear-out. Learn the ropes selling things you don't need and treat your first forays purely as a learning experience with the aim of generating a bit of pocket money. There's no better way of learning the ins and outs of the world's biggest online person-to-person marketplace.

1 | Getting to grips with eBay

> The first aspect to consider is the tools of the trade for online selling. You've probably got everything you need to start trading on eBay. A computer with web access is vital, and a fast connection to the World Wide Web will save you time. It doesn't matter whether you favour Apple Mac products or are happy with a PC: eBay and Amazon work just fine on either. However, be aware that a few of eBay's features such as Turbo Lister are not Mac compatible. Don't let this discourage you, though: other apps and programs are available that will do just the same.

Indeed, there's no reason why you couldn't run a very successful small ecommerce business from an iPad. The only limitation would be the storage of files such as images, although cloud storage might suit you for this.

CREATING DIGITAL IMAGES >

While a digital camera is essential, in the early stages of your ecommerce career the camera on your phone may well suffice. Indeed, combined with the eBay mobile app, taking photos on your smartphone can be one of the quickest ways to list an item on the site.

As you progress, an investment in the best camera you can afford will certainly reap rewards. That will probably mean a digital SLR with a great lens and a good zoom facility. Images are increasingly important in the very competitive arena of ecommerce and amateurish snaps just don't cut the mustard.

As ever more customers are buying using their mobile phones, really crisp and clear imagery can clinch the deal. And that's not only about the kit – you need expertise too, so it's well worth taking the time (maybe even taking a course) to learn how your camera works.

If you're selling as a business, for a relatively modest outlay you can establish a well-lit, fit-for-purpose photographic studio in a corner of your workspace. This will save you time and enhance your ability to produce first-class snaps for your ecommerce listings.

A flatbed scanner as well as a digital camera is a good way of capturing images if you're selling small or paper items that will fit on the screen. Scanners (especially those combined with printers so they can operate as a photocopier too) really are as cheap as chips and are a sound investment if you're selling products like postcards, stamps and jewellery.

PRINTING >

A printer is a necessity because you'll have to print out dispatch notes and other paperwork. However, one that's cheap and cheerful will be more than adequate to begin with and you probably have one of those already.

A laser printer will allow you to print many more pages a minute than the inkjet variety, at a fraction of the overall cost in the long run. The expense is easy to justify when your business is dispatching dozens of items a day and you may be able to buy one second-hand on eBay itself. Don't forget to investigate the cost of toner cartridges, which for either variety are often more than the printer itself. Also, gadgets like a special label printer to make address stickers for your parcels are dead cheap (circa £20) and very useful.

PACKING >

From your earliest days as a trader, it's a good idea to ensure you have a ready supply of packaging materials: padded envelopes, packing tape, bubble wrap and cardboard. You really can never have enough of that stuff and keeping it to hand will save you time when you dispatch your wares. It's fine to recycle material you've received, but that won't be scalable as your enterprise grows, so it's best to buy what you need in bulk to save cash. And guess what? eBay's a great place to buy packaging supplies at much better prices than you'll find in your local shops.

MOBILE APPS >

The ever-increasing use of mobile phones has hugely influenced ecommerce and what the pundits call m-commerce or mobile commerce. In essense, many people now access the web and buy online using a smartphone (such as an iPhone or Android/HTC device) and also a tablet such as an iPad. This has transformed how people buy: no longer are they shackled to their desktop or laptop. Lots of this trading happens on the move and it's increasingly becoming the norm.

You may well have a smartphone or a tablet yourself, so make sure that you get the relevant apps for your devices as one of the first steps on your ecommerce journey. On many phones such apps will be pre-loaded or you can get them via the app store for your gadget. The full array of eBay apps is showcased at:

> http://anywhere.ebay.co.uk/mobile/iphone/ebay/

Don't forget that you can get apps for PayPal, Amazon and all sorts of other ecommerce sites and services. A good way to find what's available is to visit the site in question and often you'll be given the option to download the app there and then.

You need such apps not only to use for your own purchasing, but to see what your listings look like on a mobile device

- through a buyer's eyes. If they look great, you're on the right track. But if your images are grainy or unclear, it will demonstrate that you have work to do to clinch the maximum number of sales.

> Tip: False economies

Successful ecommerce merchants stick to doing what they do best and outsource the rest. Finding ways to save time and energy will reap rewards as you develop your business. Your time is not best spent on trifles but on sourcing better stock and researching sales trends that produce profits.

When it comes to equipment, something that saves minutes every day gives you hours of extra time over the course of a year. So take the time to consider factors other than cost when investing in software and hardware.

Remember as you read this book that when your business grows in sophistication and develops over multiple channels, the tools of the ecommerce trade will need to develop with you. A powerful computer will be necessary to run sophisticated management programs, accounting software and all manner of other apps to keep your business running smoothly. You'll also need proper back-up systems so that in the event of a meltdown, you don't lose everything. (Believe me, it happens. One seller I know had to cease trading because he lost all the data on his computer.)

REGISTERING WITH eBAY >

If you haven't done so already, registering with eBay is the work of moments. The first step is to provide your personal and contact details. You need to fill in your name, address and telephone number.

It is very important that you put in correct personal details and valid contact information. If the information you provide is false, you will be suspended from eBay without warning (eBay is unforgiving here) and you will have to go through the rigmarole of confirming your identity by providing domestic bills and ID like a passport or driving licence, which can be time consuming and irritating.

eBay communicates with its members via email, so it's also important that you provide an email address to which you have regular access. You'll need to type it in twice to confirm that it's correct.

You then have to choose your User ID and password. Your User ID is a key part of your eBay personality. Take a moment to think about what you want it to be. Don't forget that as a buyer, and more importantly as a seller, your User ID says something about you and can influence people's attitude. A good name will attract other eBay members, but one with dodgy overtones might put people off trading with you. You want to make money on eBay and not provide the laughs, so choose something sober and businesslike that you'll be able to live with for a while.

> Tip: User IDs
If you have an idea for an ID and want to see if it's already been taken by someone else, use the Member Search facility to check it out. Hit the 'advanced' link at the right of the search

button at the top of every page. On the advanced search page on the left-hand side you'll see options to help you 'Find a member', where you can search for your desired User ID. If you don't find it, it's available.

Select a password that's easy for you to remember and impossible for other people to guess. Try to use a mix of letters and numbers and also include both lower- and upper-case letters. You can make the password easier to remember by using numbers as if they're letters: 'z00k33pEr' or 'Mi11icent'.

When you've completed all the sections on the Registration Form you're taken to the next page, where you're asked to accept and agree to eBay's User Agreement and Privacy Policy. You can print these out so you can peruse them more easily. Once you've agreed to the terms, eBay sends you an email, which is a way of checking that the email address you provided is correct. When you receive the email, click the 'Confirm Registration' button inside. That will take you to eBay and you'll then be a fully registered member, ready to use the site.

> Tip: Anonymous email addresses
eBay takes safety very seriously and one way it protects the people who are buying and selling on the site is to require a credit or debit card from anyone registering with an anonymous email account such as Microsoft's Outlook or Yahoo!. If you do want to register using such an account, you'll need to be prepared to provide credit or debit card information in addition to everything else.

What if my email doesn't arrive?
If you register on eBay and you don't get the confirmation email immediately, sit tight. It can take up to 24 hours to arrive. If after a day you haven't received it, it's wise to request that eBay sends it again. You can do this via the 'Confirm Registration' link on the Site Map.

If you do have to ask for your email again, the chances are that your email provider is to blame. You may have your email account security settings so high that you can only receive emails from senders pre-approved by you. If your security settings are in order and you still haven't received the email, you'll need to contact your email provider or internet service provider for advice. Emails are a significant part of selling on eBay, so you need to be sure you won't have any problems receiving them.

> Inside Information: Get the latest eBay news

I've crammed as much information as possible into the pages of this book. But as with anything on the internet, there's always something new to say and changes to report. That's why you can keep up to date with the latest eBay developments at a blog I edit: www.tamebay.com

Whether it's a change to the eBay site, my latest view on this or that, or just an update I think will be of interest, by reading the blog you can find out what's going on. It would be great to see you, so why not pop by? Also, if you want to get in touch, you can contact me directly via Tamebay. I'd love to hear from you.

Case study | Britain's first eBayer | eBay user ID: gf-attic

Graham discovered eBay in 1996, about a year after it was founded. He was one of the first Brits to start selling on the site and he's still at it today. He's a Top-rated Seller who specialises in selling antique sewing machines and other collectables.

'eBay was more of a cosy club,' he said about the early days. 'The whole concept of auctioning items online was a great novelty and provided thousands of words of interesting comment on the various news groups. Back then the vast majority of items offered for sale were collectables and used computer equipment. I also remember being able to give feedback, both positive and negative, on a whim.'

There was no eBay.co.uk back then and Graham traded on eBay.com. In fact, he still lists on the American site in US dollars because that's what his buyers like; the vast majority of his buyers are in the United States. 'I realised very early on that it takes a great leap of faith for someone to send money to a country they've never visited, to a person they don't know, for an item they haven't seen. So we've got to make it easy for our buyers.'

Graham is attracted to the worldwide customer base that eBay still offers him. He had previously sold and restored antiques with an outlet in London, but eBay's arrival on the scene was timely: the antiques business collapsed in the mid-1990s and Graham considered leaving the trade altogether. 'The advent of eBay allowed me to stay in the game but working in an entirely different way. I've lots of complaints about the way eBay has evolved into a relatively faceless giant. But it was there when I needed it. It saved my bacon.'

That worldwide audience makes eBay a particularly effective way of selling rare items. The audience and the auction also help Graham shift things he might otherwise not sell: 'I deal over a large range of collectables. And while I have expertise in certain areas, others are a closed book to me, and I would have no idea how, in a shop, to write a price ticket. With eBay auctions I don't need to. I can put on a reserve that covers my costs and let the market sort out the correct final figure.'

2 | Buying on eBay:
The research lab for eBay sellers

> The ultimate aim of this book is to get you selling and making serious money on eBay and elsewhere. First, as with any new project, it's vital to lay some foundations. And when it comes to eBay, you'll learn many valuable lessons if you initially get to grips with eBay as a buyer, rather than a seller.

10 THINGS YOU LEARN AS AN eBAY BUYER >

Your time as a buyer is a vital nursery for your emerging eBay selling career. If you keep your eyes and mind open, there are 10 key things to discover as you bid and BIN.

1 > eBay is not really about auctions
Every time eBay is in the papers, it's dubbed an 'auction site'. And while that's a commonly held view, it's a description that's no longer true. That's how eBay started and it does still host stacks of auctions, particularly for antiques, collectables and oodles of second-hand stuff. But today it's not the majority of what eBay does.

    eBay is now predominantly a marketplace that sells new items using the Buy It Now system. Indeed, a growing number of its sellers are professional and plenty of big retailers are in on the act, including high-street names like Argos and Boden. And the most popular categories these days include consumer electronics, fashion, cars and homewares.

2 > Sexy listings sell
Cruising around eBay will help you develop a discerning eye for a good listing. So as you shop, make a mental note (maybe even make an actual note) of what you like, remember the things that stood out and enticed you to look at an item, the features

and approaches that you found attractive and persuaded you to buy.

There's such an abundance of items for sale and such an embarrassment of choice that you won't be slow to realise that the item itself, its price and P&P, isn't always – or in fact often – what decides the day. A deal is usually clinched by a cocktail of a brilliantly honed listing, a well-respected seller and winning pictures and descriptions. Basically, sexy listings sell.

And while you're at it, scribble down the things that turn you off. What sends you running from a particular item? Screeds of petty text, annoying rules and shoddy snaps, I bet. Those are the unsexy things that you should remember to avoid.

> Tip

When you're looking at other listings you will notice that there are lots of eBay-specific terms and acronyms in use across the site. Thankfully, eBay has provided a glossary (http://pages. ebay.co.uk/help/account/glossary.html) as well as a guide to acronyms in its help section (http://pages.ebay.co.uk/help/ account/acronyms.html).

3 > Feedback and Detailed Seller Ratings are crucial

eBay is justifiably famous for and proud of its unique feedback system. It's how buyers and sellers rate each other and it helps you decide if you want to buy from a seller. But as your first forays onto eBay will reveal, feedback is really quite complicated and nuanced. It's not merely a case of judging the percentage of positives, because just about everyone has more than 98% positive feedback.

What you also need to consider are those niggling little Detailed Seller Ratings (DSRs), which show what buyers think about specific aspects of a seller's performance.

Buyers rate sellers from 1 to 5 stars on the accuracy of their descriptions, the speed and quality of their communication, the speediness of their dispatching and how reasonable their P&P costs are. Decoding all these symbols takes a bit of time, but it's a vital skill to acquire.

4 > Best Match can make the difference

One other reason DSRs matter is that eBay uses them to order how items are found in search. How eBay decides what to show buyers first when they do a search on the site is a closely guarded secret over which the company keeps a sphinx-like silence. However, what we do know is that a seller's DSRs are critical in regard to their position in what's called Best Match.

eBay prefers sellers who are top rated (see below) with great DSRs. It likes items with Free P&P or Fast & Free dispatch. Best Match also appears to push multiple item listings on which there have been successful sales up the list; auctions too seem to bob up as they end. Performing well in Best Match will be essential to your business success, so getting to grips with how it works is very important.

5 > Top-rated Sellers stand out

Lots of sellers have achieved the coveted Top-rated Seller status on eBay. This has replaced the old PowerSeller system and offers very real benefits to sellers. Not least of the perks is that a TRS will get a boost in Best Match and obtain greater visibility.

How do you become a TRS? Happy customers! If over time you satisfy the buyers, get consistently 5-star DSRs and very, very few complaints from buyers and also have a high level of eBay policy compliance, then you too can become a TRS.

But remember, eBay giveth and eBay taketh away. If your standards slip, that useful and valuable badge will be taken away without any apology.

6 > Postage costs count

Some eBay sellers have lost the plot on postage costs – you often see quite small items with sky-high postage charges attached. Cheap or free postage can give you a real boost in search and attract buyers, making it one of the most competitive areas of a listing. Even so, many sellers display exorbitant carriage costs or don't give you any information up front (which is probably worse). Other sellers, who could easily send a parcel with a weight up to 5kg for something like £5 with a courier, greatly limit their pool of potential buyers by stating 'collection only'.

Learn to appreciate postage costs from a buyer's perspective rather than that of a seller. It's a whole different way to look at them and will spur you on to make the costs you offer as attractive as possible.

7 > PayPal pays

PayPal is ubiquitous. Get to know this way of sending and receiving money – it has loads of useful features for buyers.

8 > Some sellers are shoddy

Buying can be trying. Just a few weeks ago I bought a book on eBay. I chose a Top-rated Seller and paid a fair price for first-class postage; the parcel took a week to arrive. That isn't unusual. Many sellers are stuck in a rut and don't realise how demanding consumers are. Amazon has led the way here, most of the time delivering the goods the next day or the one after. eBay buyers have come to expect a similar service and have become impatient.

9 > Buyers compete

It's not only sellers who are competing with each other on eBay – buyers are too. In the bidding wars to grab a bargain or in their quest to buy items with BIN, there are a lot of sharp elbows. Use your own buying experience to think about how you can turn that to your advantage as a seller.

10 > Mobile is on the move

The future of eBay lies with the mobile phone and tablets like the iPad. It doesn't seem outrageous to predict a future where people don't buy online with what we now call laptops and desktop computers, but instead use only mcommerce. The size of the potential market is huge. Learn as a buyer how eBay works on these devices so you can utilise this information to your advantage as a seller.

FEEDBACK AND DSRS >

Feedback is your friend when deciding whether a certain seller or buyer is the kind of person you want to do business with. The Seller Information Box on the Item Description page gives you plenty of information, but you need to unravel it.

Look for a positive feedback score of 98% or above. Remember that a high total isn't automatically a guarantee in itself. If you want to find out about a seller, or if you're curious about a buyer, click on the feedback total to find out more about their eBay history.

But Feedback is so much more than a percentage and a total. The Detailed Seller Ratings on the Member Profile let you know how swift, honest and conscientious a certain seller is (DSRs aren't applicable to buyers). You're looking for scores of between 4 and 5 across the board.

Detailed Seller Ratings (last 12 months)		?
Criteria	**Average rating**	**Number of ratings**
Item as described	★★★★★	17
Communication	★★★★★	18
Dispatch time	★★★★★	16
Postage and packaging charges	★★★★★	19

DSRs give you the details about a member's previous activities on eBay and more information to use to form a judgement. The stars you see should be as close to 5 as possible. If you're buying a rare antique, say, you want to know how full and honest a seller's description is. If you're in a hurry, fast dispatch counts.

If there's any negative feedback on the profile, you want to find out what it's for. Someone with 1000 feedbacks has clearly had many successful trades with many different members, but a closer examination will reveal whether a trader has received complaints. A few negative feedbacks here and there are pretty much inevitable for members with a lot of feedback, but sometimes even excellent feedback totals conceal those with less than enviable reputations.

If you're looking into a seller, you can check the items they've sold recently and examine the feedback that was left. If a seller has already received good feedback for an item similar to the one you want to bid on, then you can probably bid with confidence. You benefit from the same effect when you're selling items yourself.

> Tip: Feedback

It's easy to take false comfort from the fact that a seller has 20,000 positive feedbacks or to judge someone too harshly because they only have 99.7% positive. Every Member Profile tells a story and as with any source of information, oversimplification can render the information misleading.

A bumper feedback total and a very high percentage can actually disguise a seller who's selling many thousands of items a month and yet leaving several hundred buyers a month unhappy. Equally, one unfair negative left for a seller with only a few hundred feedbacks can be a disproportionately big blot on their copybook. If you really want to unleash the power of feedback, it's worth moving beyond a quick glance and digesting the information in detail to help you make the right decisions.

Repeat feedback

When you see a feedback score by a member's User ID, the number is a tally of the unique members who have left a positive

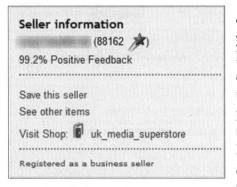

Seller information
(88162 ⭐)
99.2% Positive Feedback

Save this seller
See other items
Visit Shop: 🛒 uk_media_superstore

Registered as a business seller

comment. It doesn't tell you how many buyers have gone back again and again to buy from the same seller – if people do go back for more, that's a good sign. To see how many repeat buyers a seller is getting, go to the Member Profile and look for 'All positive feedback received'. If this number is higher than the unique score, it means the seller has repeat bidders. Obviously, if the repeat score is very high, it means that people keep going back to the seller to buy.

Check items being sold

What's the feedback for? You need to check that the feedback is for selling and hopefully for items like the one you want to buy. Click on the item numbers by the feedback comments to see what the feedback is for.

Feedback profile

(124216 ⭐) me 🔲
Positive Feedback (last 12 months): 99.5%
[How is Feedback percentage calculated?]
Member since: 10-Nov-08 in United Kingdom
Registered as a Business Seller

This member is an **eBay Top-rated seller**

✔ Consistently receives highest buyer ratings
✔ Dispatches items quickly
✔ Has earned a track record of excellent service
Learn more

Recent Feedback ratings (last 12 months) [?]

	1 month	6 months	12 months
➕ Positive	3480	26014	61203
⭕ Neutral	21	186	372
➖ Negative	15	150	297

Detailed Seller Ratings (last 12 months) [?]

Criteria	Average rating	Number of ratings
Item as described	★★★★★	46174
Communication	★★★★★	51555
Dispatch time	★★★★★	46058
Postage and packaging charges	★★★★★	48770

SAFE TRADING CHECKLIST >

To make sure you stay secure, here are five questions to ask yourself before you bid on something.

1 > Do you know what you're buying?

Never place a bid in haste and make sure that you're buying a genuine article. Read the small print and make sure that the item's exactly what you want. It's always worth researching expensive items thoroughly using the internet and other sources so you make the right purchase.

2 > Do you trust the seller?

As a buyer, you have lots of sources of information to help you make a sound judgement. If you don't get the information you need to make a choice, then think about finding another seller. Take a few minutes to check out the other items the seller has sold. Do they have a track record of selling items similar to the one you want to buy? Have they got happy customers?

That's why buying from Top-rated Sellers is recommended if you're wary of spending a lot of cash. As we've seen, they have a proven track record of providing excellent customer service and playing safe. Business sellers are also required to publish their contact details, which can be a reassurance. If you want to make sure, feel free to contact the seller directly.

3 > Is the seller truthful?

While you may be very happy to buy from abroad, be wary of sellers who claim to be in Britain but are in fact in another country. Not only is it against eBay rules to claim you're in the UK when you're not, doing so can be a hallmark of a dodgy seller. Double check the seller's location. If the postage seems very high and the price of the item very low, be wary too.

4 > Can you get your money back if you need to?

Fraudulent sellers don't have the items they're claiming to sell and want to trick you into sending money you can't retrieve. Do not pay using cash or instant money transfers such as Western Union or MoneyGram. Paying by PayPal, especially if the seller is guaranteed under the PayPal Buyer Protection scheme, is the best and safest method.

5 > Can you return the goods if you aren't happy?

Many of the best sellers allow you to return the goods you buy on eBay. Check out the seller's returns policy at the bottom of the View Item page to see whether you can return what you buy if you want to. You may have to pay return carriage or send the item back within a set period, but it's good for peace of mind to be able to do so. Certainly, if you're buying something of high value, you want to know that you can send it back if you want. If a seller doesn't take returns, you might want to try finding one who does.

> Tip: The Safety Centre

eBay sometimes gets a bad rap for being an unsafe place to trade. This is usually not much more than hot air and media

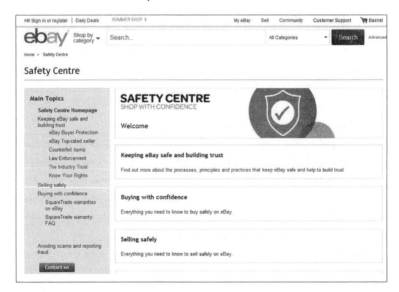

sensationalism. Of course, sometimes bad things happen, but not as frequently as you might expect.

The best defence is information and getting tooled up with the right advice on staying safe. For this you need the eBay Safety Centre. It's packed with very useful, easy to digest help on staying safe on eBay:

> http://pages.ebay.co.uk/safetycentre/index.html

Case study | Advice from an old hand | eBay user ID: sean_coolness

Sean got started on eBay by accident. He had a loft full of brand new but slightly out-of-date computer bits and pieces. A friend had just discovered eBay and recommended that Sean have a go. 'My first listing,' says Sean, 'was for a Pentium Pro PS2 motherboard. It sold very well and made four times more than I expected! That gave me the incentive to start listing away. I haven't looked back since.'

Sean now sells on eBay full time and makes his living from the site. He runs his business using two selling accounts. He has discovered that that it's a good idea when trying to create a good brand to have an ID relevant to what's for sale. That's why he has one ID with which he sells motorbikes and a secondary ID for selling bike accessories and sundries.

He told me, 'This actually gives me two completely different types of account. One account is low-volume, high-ticket items, the other is high-volume, lower-value items, so I get to see both ends of the sales spectrum as a seller.' He is also a keen buyer: 'I'm a collector of first-edition books. I have now managed to get full sets by three different authors; that would have been very difficult before the advent of eBay.'

He found it easy to transform his selling from a hobby to a business. He comments, 'I simply listed more to sell more. It's a bit of basic selling really. If you only have five items listed, you can only sell five items. But if you have one hundred items listed, you have a lot more potential for sales.'

Sean reckons that honesty is the best policy: 'I think the most basic of things that any seller needs to know is one of eBay's core values, be honest! Be honest in your description, in your postage costs, in your location and in any emails. eBay buyers have an amazing knack of rooting out the bad sellers very quickly. In most part by the feedback system, a bad seller's reputation is instantly visible. So be an honest seller. It doesn't matter if the item is marked, broken or stained, all that matters is that you are honest!'

And honesty is also vital if something goes wrong: 'Don't go into a panic when you make a mistake. If you have listed something which has sold and you then discover a problem, don't start telling little porkie pies. Simply communicate honestly with your buyer and explain the issue to them: a vast majority will understand that we are all human and we occasionally make mistakes.'

For beginners, Sean has two nuggets of advice: do your research and be ready to face up to change. Getting to know eBay well before you take the plunge will 'save you a lot of time and money later on. Find out if your widget has a market on eBay and at what price. Learn the sell-through and conversion rates for that widget and work out if there is enough margin in it for you to list that item two, three and even four times! Find out what colours sell best and what times and days are best. It's back to school to do your homework first, but you will save yourself a lot of pain later on.'

And 'be very aware of just how quickly things can change on eBay. Learn to plan ahead, have a strategy and alternatives. You need to be able to adapt very quickly if you want to stay ahead of the game.'

3 | Preparing to sell on eBay

> You've cracked the eBay buying challenge – now it's time to start selling. There are just a few bits of paperwork to attend to before you can be unleashed on the marketplace.

REGISTERING AS A SELLER WITH eBAY >

Before you can list your first item you need to create a Seller's Account. You fill in an online form and provide information that verifies that you are who you say you are. Click 'Sell' in the Navigation Bar on the eBay.co.uk homepage, then on the Sell Hub you need to click 'Sell My Item' and sign in again.

---

ebay

Register with eBay

It's your typical registration - it's free and fairly simple to complete.
Register your business today to bid, buy or sell on eBay. Already registered or want to make change

Q If you're not planning to run a business on eBay, use standard registration.
Q Car dealers should register here.
(Learn more about registering as a car dealer.)

Tell us about your business - All fields are required

Business name

Business type
[Select business type ▼]

Salutation
[- ▼]

When you sit down to create your Seller's Account, make sure that you have the following close to hand:

> A credit or debit card. You can choose to use a Visa or MasterCard credit card or a debit card of some sort.

> A statement that corresponds to the debit or credit card. You need to enter the postal address relating to the card you're intending to use. It's best to have the bill to hand so you can be sure to enter the information accurately.

eBay will then ask you to verify your personal details and how you want to pay your eBay fees. You can choose to use the credit or debit card you have just entered, a direct debit or PayPal. PayPal is usually the easiest option.

REGISTERING YOUR BUSINESS WITH eBAY >

If you're a business trading on eBay, you must let the site know that. The selling regulations also require that some of your information, such as address and VAT number if relevant, is available to buyers.

To register as a business, visit:

> http://pages.ebay.co.uk/services/registration/ businesslanding.html

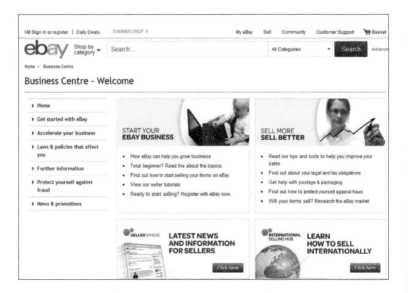

This page of legal guidance for business sellers is also invaluable:

> http://pages.ebay.co.uk/help/policies/business.html

Plus there is a wealth of info at the eBay Business Centre:

> http://pages.ebay.co.uk/businesscentre/

REGISTERING ON PAYPAL AS A BUSINESS USER >

PayPal also likes to know if you're a business user, and there are perks available if you are. The most important service PayPal offers to volume sellers is discounted fees. If you're accepting more than £1500 a month in payments, you can get a reduction in fees, although you don't get this automatically, you have to apply.

To register, log into PayPal and click the Merchant Services link on your account page.

4 | Deciding what to sell

> Most of the eBay sellers I've met over the years are generous, chatty souls who are always sharing tips and chatting about customers or eBay's latest cock-up. But if there's one topic that makes them clam up and leads to blank, unresponsive faces, it's the issue of sourcing stock to sell.

You'll never get an answer to the question: 'So where do you get your stock?' And indeed, why should you? Stock is the holy grail of any retail business. It's a problem you'll have to resolve yourself, but here are some useful pointers to get you started.

HAVING A CLEAR-OUT >

The best way to start selling on eBay is to sell some things you already own. This has several key benefits. First, it doesn't cost you anything and you almost certainly have something you don't need languishing around your house. Secondly, there's no paperwork. When you sell your own stuff the tax authorities can't poke their noses in: you don't have to pay tax on any money you make selling your own belongings.

Start with small things that you don't mind letting go for a few quid. Books, DVDs, CDs, computer games and the like are ideal. They're dead easy to list and and they also pose no real challenge to post. Limit these first sales to the UK too for hassle-free selling. This is a learning experience and there's no need to complicate matters unnecessarily by having to ship goods overseas or deal with customs or foreign language speakers.

You might have a valuable family heirloom, something highly collectable or a big-ticket item that you want to flog at some point, but leave that a while: you won't get the price you want if you don't have some feedback and list it properly. eBay's also a great venue for selling your car, but I suggest you leave finding out about that huge category too until you've had some experience.

If you don't have anything you want to sell (and I simply don't believe you if that's the case), there are other ways you can source stuff to sell. It would be hard to run a full-time business using the following sources as the primary ways to obtain stock, but for hobby sellers or those starting off they have some merit.

CAR BOOT SALES >

In your local area there will doubtless be hundreds of car boot sales to choose from every year. So get out and about and ascertain which are worth going to again and again and which are an outlet for hopeless hopefuls selling the tat and detritus that nobody really wants to buy.

Making a handsome profit from car boot sale purchases takes some skill and discipline. Don't forget that you'll be competing with dealers, professional traders and maybe even other eagle-eyed eBay sellers as you patrol the stalls.

Remember three things that will help you out in that muddy field or school car park:

> Get there quickly – all the best stuff will be snapped up by the early birds and if you arrive later you'll find it tougher to uncover the gems.
> Cash is king at car boots – make sure you have a fat wad of the finest folding so you can pay up there and then, as very few traders take cards or cheques.
> You have to haggle – never take the seller's first price, as even knocking a few quid off the asking price can make all the difference when you come to sell something on.

CHARITY SHOPS >

It used to be the case that the charity shops on every high street provided a rich seam of brilliant bargains for industrious eBay sellers to grab and sell on to happy buyers all over the world at bumper mark-ups. However, charity shops have upped their game and become more savvy. The result is that treasures that previously cost pence will now set you back pounds. It also won't surprise you to learn that some charity shops are selling on eBay themselves.

Nevertheless, don't dismiss this option out of hand. With a bit of legwork and a keen eye, you can still find brilliant things to sell at a profit. Establish a round of charity shops that are off the beaten track to get hold of the best stuff. Shops in posher areas often have the best swag.

It can also be worth striking up relationships with the managers of your local shops. Or you might find that they offer volunteers first dibs on their donations, so it could be time to volunteer your services. Otherwise, just keep your nose to the ground and scour the local shops regularly and you'll be able to pick up some valuable stock.

SCAVENGING >

This idea won't be for everyone, but what could be more satisfying than selling something you got for free at a handsome profit? In the words of Dire Straits, it's money for nothing.

Skip dipping is the first option. It's fair game to grab what you like out of a skip as long as you ask permission, and you'll be amazed at what people throw away.

You can also scavenge by using the classified ads. Take a look in your local rag or scour online resources such as Gumtree and Freecycle looking for the magic words 'free to collector'. Often people just want rid of the clutter and are grateful if someone's willing to stop by and take it away.

And maybe you could consider advertising. If you have wheels and time, offer a free house clearing or clutter take-away service. Who knows what treasures you might find?

SOURCING REGULAR STOCK >

To make serious money on eBay, you need a solid and plentiful supply of stock. To locate that regular supplier (or even more than one), you'll need to put in a bit of legwork and not be shy.

Chris Dawson of Tamebay is an eBay seller of more than a decade's standing and thinks that the fact it's tricky to locate suppliers is one of the benefits of – and incentives to – doing it right.

'Sourcing stock, while often seeming impossible, is simply a case of putting in the hard work,' says Chris. 'Every product has a manufacturer and if you can identify who makes the product you may be able to buy direct. Some manufacturers don't sell direct, in which case they'll be quite happy to tell you who their distributors are.

'Trade fairs such as the annual Spring Fair and Autumn Fair can be a great way to meet manufacturers and distributors in person, but in reality phone calls to the right person can frequently open all the doors you need. Don't be afraid to make initial test purchases from competitors, often the item itself will have revealing information and I've even received products packed in an outer box carrying the UK importer's contact details.

'Finding a great source of stock won't be easy, but you should take heart from that – if it was easy everyone would be doing it. The harder it is for you to find and build a relationship with a supplier, the harder it will be for your competitors to do likewise.'

> Tip: Spring Fair

Usually held at the beginning of February, the Spring Fair at the NEC near Birmingham is a very good place to start if you want ideas and inspiration for what to sell. It's an absolutely massive trade fair where you can meet and chat to suppliers and browse all manner of products and goods – there are something like 3000 exhibitors and 300,000 items on display.

Covering everything from gifts to fashion, jewellery, homewares, toys and even specific Christmas gifts, Spring Fair is a massive showcase of what is likely to be in the shops in the months to come. It's an opportunity for you to make some contacts and get chatting with suppliers, manufacturers and wholesalers. Check out the website:

> http://www.springfair.com/sfi/website/Home.aspx

Wholesalers and importers

Wholesalers and importers are where most serious eBayers get their stock. These are businesses that specialise in selling items directly to retailers in bulk at a price lower than you would expect in a shop. They don't typically sell directly to the public and they will sell in massive bundles: by the pallet load, in batches of 100 or just by weight. Track down such companies in your local area using Google or the Yellow Pages. Be prepared to prove your business bona fides too: they will want to know that you're reputable. But do persevere, as these people are worth working with.

The following two websites are absolutely brilliant and will be massively helpful as you try to source great stock to sell:

> The Wholesale Forum is a vibrant community that connects you with wholesalers all around the world. It claims to have 100,000 contacts and I know a lot of eBay sellers swear by the forum and what it does. Make a beeline for
> > http://www.wholesaleforum.com/discuss/
> The Wholesaler is a UK-based directory of wholesalers based all over the country. It is organised by region and also product

type. It's fantastically useful and free, so head over to
> http://www.thewholesaler.co.uk/

> Tip
There's another useful site called stockshifters.com, which is
essentially an online wholesaler where you can buy goods to
sell on eBay. You will doubtless find better prices elsewhere,
but it's a good place to consider as you start selling. More and
more online wholesalers are popping up and one new kid on
the block, Boffer.co.uk, is also worth checking out.

Going straight to the manufacturers

One of the most profitable sources of eBay stock, but also one
of the more risky avenues and certainly one that's hard to break
into, is to deal directly with the manufacturers. They sell directly
to retailers and sometimes will do deals with reputable eBay sellers. This is also where you should start casting your eyes overseas
to find makers of goods – and no one makes a bigger range of
goods than the ever so industrious Chinese. Locating manufacturers will take some real sleuthing, nevertheless.

Check out sites like alibaba.com to see whether you can
source products from Asia at a good price. Be warned, though,
long-distance trading carries potential dangers and you'll likely
be waiting months for the goods to arrive on... well... a slow boat
from China. It's tricky, it's challenging but when it works, it's a
real earner.

End-of-line products and liquidations

This is the stuff that other people haven't been able to sell,
whether a supermarket or shop or indeed a wholesaler. Disposing
of any unsold goods involves a cost and often you'll be able to get
your hands on the leftovers at a knock-down rate. The box might
be damaged and it's likely to be a mixed bag, but when you buy
stock by the pallet it can be very cheap indeed. You'll need to cultivate relationships to make sure you get the good stuff and not
the humdinger lots.

Buying at auctions

Auctions come in all shapes and sizes and can be a great way of getting your hands on brilliant stock to sell on eBay. The trouble is that they can be rather daunting for the newcomer and every auction house has different rules and conventions. Most common are the traditional auction houses, often found in market towns, which specialise in household goods, house clearances, antiques and the like. Often you can find boxes of lovely stuff selling for just a few quid.

There are other types of auctions too. Airport operators often auction left luggage, although you don't get to check the contents of a suitcase and it's more a case (ahem) of pot luck. The police also appoint auctioneers to sell unclaimed items. Don't forget motor auctions and also commercial sales. The best place to find out what's on in your area is your local newspaper or the internet.

Understanding how a particular auction house works is vital. Find out in advance if you have to register to participate or if it's a free-for-all. Make sure that you have adequate funds and transport for the items you buy. Most establishments expect you to pay up immediately and take your goods away sharpish. Check out the costs at that particular auction and beware the buyer's premium and VAT. The buyer's premium is likely to be 10–15% of the sale price, but it could be as high as 20%. With all the extras added on, your bargain may not look quite so promising.

MAKING YOUR OWN STOCK >

It's always satisfying to turn an activity you do for fun or love into a lucrative sideline. If you have a craft, skill or hobby that means you can make items to sell, such as greeting cards, clothing, gifts or anything similar, consider turning it into a business.

Take a look through eBay for inspiration and you'll be amazed at the creativity and industry of the eBay community.

There's original artwork (of varying quality), sculpture, ceramics, simple craft creations and all manner of other ingenious products.

The thing to bear in mind, if you embark on this route, is not to get carried away. Be realistic about the prices you set for your treasures as you're building up a feedback reputation, and don't forget to factor in all the expenses you incur when you make your wares. The aim here is to make a bit of money while still enjoying your hobby. Don't turn something you love doing into a drudge because you're chasing profits too hard.

SELLING FOR OTHER PEOPLE >

By the time you've read this book and mastered the techniques of selling on eBay, you'll be an ecommerce expert. You'll know everything there is to know about selling on eBay for profit and that information is a valuable commodity in itself. It also gives you an opportunity to put your new genius for eBaying to good use by selling for other people.

Tout for business among your friends and colleagues, advertise your services and let everyone know that you're willing to take the sting out of listing things for sale on eBay for a reasonable fee. Value items, write winning item descriptions and whip out the digital camera to produce amazing snaps so their goodies get the prices they deserve.

Clarify with the owner, right from the start, what your terms are. Get them to name the minimum amount they're willing to sell the item for and agree a fee for yourself. That could be a fixed sum or commission based on the selling price of the item.

Where possible, plump to sell bigger-ticket items so it's worth your while to do the selling. And don't forget to factor in all your costs, including eBay and PayPal fees and (most importantly) your time.

> Tip: Space costs money

Whatever you decide to sell, stock that isn't moving is a problem. You may have high hopes for that wonderful widget but eBay's buying public may disagree. It's better to get rid of the stock at a reduced price than to cling on to it in the vain hope of making a fortune. There's great merit in a clearance sale, which means you can liquidate stock and transform it into ready money that can be invested in new stock that will turn a profit.

Remember that storing stock that isn't shifting costs you money. Until it sells your cash is tied up, but don't forget the costs of storage too. Most importantly, for most online traders space is at a premium, and if your valuable storage space is occupied by old stock, you can't buy new stuff in to flog.

5 | Getting ready for a successful eBay sale

Once you've registered as a seller, you can list something to sell on eBay by entering your details into the Sell Your Item form. You need to provide all the relevant information you want in your listing so that eBay can build the page for you. If you've prepared all the information you require in advance, you'll be able to fill in the Sell Your Item form quickly and easily.

Delighting potential customers through your item information is something of an art form that you'll need to master. Here are the things you should think about in advance of listing your item – the component parts of an eBay sale.

FINDABILITY >

eBay has a complex search engine that's changing all the time. To help people find your items, you need to provide all of the key information. This comprises three vital aspects: your item category, your item title and what is termed Item Specifics.

Choosing a category

As you will remember from your experiences as a buyer, the items for sale on eBay are organised in a category structure rather like in a library.

The fact that there are thousands of categories on eBay is a mixed blessing. On the one hand, it means you're certain to find one that's just right for the item you want to sell, but on the other, it might take you a few moments to find it. Choosing the right category is very important, nevertheless, because it helps buyers locate your item and helps eBay provide the right items to buyers.

There are three ways to find the best category for the item you want to sell. The first is to browse the full list of categories. You can do this by clicking on the 'Shop by category' link by the eBay logo on the website homepage and pretending you're a buyer

All Categories			
Antiques	**Art**	**Baby**	**Books, Comics & Magazines**
Antique Clocks	Artists (Self-Representing)	Baby Bathing/ Grooming	Accessories
Antique Furniture	Canvas/ Giclee Prints	Baby Books	Antiquarian & Collectable
Antiquities	Contemporary Paintings	Baby Carriers/ Backpacks	Audio Books
Architectural Antiques	Drawings	Baby Changing & Nappies	Children's & Young Adults
More ▾	More ▾	More ▾	More ▾
Business, Office & Industrial	**Cameras & Photography**	**Cars, Motorcycles & Vehicles**	**Clothes, Shoes & Accessories**
Agriculture/ Farming	Camcorders	Aircraft & Aviation	Dancewear & Accessories
Building Materials & Supplies	Digital Cameras	Boats & Watercraft	Fancy Dress & Period Costume
Businesses For Sale	Camera & Photo Accessories	Campers, Caravans & Motorhomes	Kids' Clothes, Shoes & Accs.
Electrical & Test Equipment	Film Photography	Cars	Men's Accessories
More ▾	More ▾	More ▾	More ▾
Coins	**Collectables**	**Computers/Tablets & Networking**	**Crafts**
Banknotes	Advertising	iPads/Tablets & eBook Readers	Beads
Bullion/Bars	Animals	iPad/Tablet/eBook Accessories	Cake Decorating
Coins	Animation	Laptops & Netbooks	Candle & Soap Making
Historical Medals/ Medallions	Autographs	Desktops & All-in-Ones	Cardmaking & Scrapbooking
More ▾	More ▾	More ▾	More ▾
Dolls & Bears	**DVDs, Films & TV**	**Events Tickets**	**Garden & Patio**
Dolls	DVDs & Blu-rays	Cinema Tickets	Barbecuing & Outdoor Heating
Doll Accessories	Film Stock	Comedy Tickets	Bird Baths/ Feeders/ Tables
Dolls' Houses	LaserDiscs	Concert Tickets	Fencing
Dolls' House Miniatures	UMDs	Experiences	Fertiliser/ Soil Improvement
More ▾	More ▾	More ▾	More ▾

looking for your particular item. The second option is to search for an item similar to the one you want to sell and see where other sellers are listing it. You can do this via eBay's search engine, using the Search box found at the top right of most eBay pages.

In addition, once you're on the Sell Your Item form, if you give eBay an idea of what you're selling you'll get suggested categories based on other items listed on the site. This may be the easiest option.

You can list your item in two categories if you like, but if you do this, don't forget that your listing fees will be doubled (although not the Final Value Fee). It's not a sure-fire way to succeed either, so think hard about doing this – those extra fees add up. Before you pony up extra listing fees, it's better to choose a really good first category and hone your title so buyers can find you in Search.

Crafting an amazing Item Title

Your Item Title and Item Description are where you get the opportunity to show off what you're selling and persuade potential customers that it's something they want to buy. If a buyer is interested in your Item Title, they're more likely to click on it to find out more.

	Doctor Dr Who 2013 Sonic Screwdriver Re-Issue 3rd 4th 10th River Songs Future ⊙ Top-rated seller		**£14.29** ⌐Buy It Now + £3.00 postage
	DOCTOR WHO The 11th ELEVENTH Dr 5in figure Matt Smith + Sonic Screwdriver ⊙ Top-rated seller	10m left Today 19:59	**£8.49** 3 bids + £2.79 postage
	Doctor Who - 3.75" Action Figure Series 7 - THE DOCTOR - "BRAND NEW" ⊙ Top-rated seller		**£6.99** ⌐Buy It Now + £2.25 postage

The Item Title functions as the name of the item you're selling and is what buyers see first when searching or browsing. Therefore you need to ensure that it's as descriptive and eye-catching as possible so that buyers will be interested enough to look more closely. You only have limited space for your Item Title and to make effective use of the space you need to be inventive and precise.

If you were selling a Harry Potter book, you could have a title that simply read 'Harry Potter Book'. However, that wouldn't stand out from the thousands of other Harry Potter books for sale. In order to give yourself an edge, you need to think about what makes your item special and then distil the most important details into a small space. Which Harry Potter book is it? Which edition? Is it a hardback or a paperback? What kind of condition is the book in?

For instance, if you were lucky enough to have a first-edition, signed copy of *Harry Potter and the Chamber of Secrets* in mint condition, the Item Title could read 'Harry Potter Chamber of Secrets 1st Ed Signed J K Rowling Mint'.

Whatever you're selling, the Item Title should consist of words a buyer is likely to search for. Avoid meaningless or vague terms like 'old', 'good', 'nice' or 'interesting', because they're not the kind of term that people normally use when searching eBay. Stick to factual words that describe the item precisely, such as the brand, size or type. If it's of an era or style such as Georgian or Art Deco or Retro, include this term, as many people will use it to search.

Item Specifics

On the Sell Your Item form, the Item Specifics section is presented as a series of tick boxes and drop down menus that look like hard work and are easy to skip over. Don't ignore them. They are vital to your selling success, because eBay increasingly uses them to present the right items to buyers.

In Fashion categories Item Specifics will relate to sizes, colours and styles. If you're selling CDs, DVDs or the like, you'll be asked to express a genre, condition and format. Every category area is different and the Item Specifics have been honed to suit.

When you list an item, enter as many details as you can and make them accurate. They're as important as the keywords in your title. It's a great opportunity to outperform the competition, as many sellers still don't bother with this part of the form, so take a few minutes to enter them and you'll be sitting pretty.

PICTURES >

The dawn of mobile buying using an iPad or smartphone is leading to more and more people buying on the strength of the images in a listing alone. Buyers are also more demanding these days, which means that top-notch, multiple images of your item have never been more important,.

Remember that buyers on eBay don't get the opportunity to handle or examine the item they're purchasing until they receive it through the post, so by providing a picture you give them the opportunity to see as much of the item as possible online before they bid. eBay sellers agree that pictures encourage buyers to bid with more confidence.

It doesn't really matter how you generate the image as long as it's enticing: a mobile phone camera, a top-of-the range digital camera or even a scanner is fine, as I described in Chapter 1, 'Getting to grips with eBay'. What matters is the result.

Before you complete the Sell Your Item form you need to have the relevant images saved on your computer and ready to upload to the website. eBay prefers images in the JPEG (.jpg) format. Photos taken on an iPhone are already in this format; if yours are something different, you can change it using a free online image convertor such as CoolUtils.

When composing the images, make sure you think of the buyer and stick to the following guidelines.

Showing your item off

Ensure that the image you produce is sharp and in focus; blurred photos don't impress. Consider what the buyer wants to see. If you're selling a book, for instance, is the front cover preferable or would a shot of the inside be more useful? Will a buyer appreciate a close-up image of the markings or serial number if relevant?

Record collectors often value a close-up of the label on the record itself rather than merely the sleeve.

If you're selling an item in its original box, then taking the item out to photograph is usually best – unless of course this means that the item is worthless because it's been opened – rather than offering a view of some cardboard.

Composing a useful image

Photograph your item from the most appropriate aspect, remembering that the obvious picture may not be the most useful to a potential buyer. Good lighting can also make a world of difference.

The setting and background of the image are important too: avoid photographing your item in a way that distracts from it or causes confusion. Use a blank background, perhaps a sheet or cloth. Make sure that your item is the central feature of the picture.

Using multiple images

eBay lets you use up to four images on each listing free of charge, so don't scrimp on the visuals. The sales you'll achieve are worth the effort.

ITEM DESCRIPTION >

Provide as many details as you can about the item and its condition. Again, put yourself in a buyer's shoes and imagine what you would want to know if you were considering placing a bid or BIN. Talk the item up. Leave the buyer in no doubt that this is the item they want and give them reasons to place a bid.

Be creative and don't be afraid to be personal. If the item's unusual or rare, explain how you got hold of it. Go into as much detail as you can.

Make sure that you include keywords that are right for your item. One seller I know has been selling bed linen for a while and making a good living, shifting a lot of stock. Obviously, he lists most of his items in the same categories, so he was intrigued when he checked out Completed Items to see what other sellers were doing. He discovered that he wasn't including the most popular relevant keyword in his titles – when he added it his sales rocketed. You should do the same to make sure you aren't missing out on a key search term.

Don't just include all the plus points – if there's damage or something that affects the quality of the item, mention that too. Failure to disclose something now could result in negative feedback later.

Imagine you have a rare Doctor Who video for sale. A hastily assembled description would read: 'Dr Who Video "Shada". Rare, in almost perfect condition.'

That Item Description would suffice, but a few extra moments honing the description could reap bigger rewards:

'Dr Who video "Shada" BBCV 4814. This classic Tom Baker adventure, also starring Lalla Ward as Romana II, was written by Douglas Adams and is set in Cambridge. Never originally completed for broadcast in 1978 due to BBC strikes, the fragments that do exist have been linked by superb and often bizarre commentary from Baker. This adventure is now considered a classic by Who fans and the 1992 video is highly sought after. The item is in almost perfect condition with a small scuff on the spine of the video and comes complete with the script book as originally released. The video is in the PAL format and is not compatible with American (NTSC) video machines. An absolute must to complete any Whovian's video collection.'

Although you have the option to give further details later, it's wise to include some information in the Item Description about payment and postage. Explain briefly what payment methods you're willing to accept and what the postage costs will be.

Be careful about misusing jargon. Books, records and stamps in particular have a whole host of specialist terms that dealers use to describe items. If you misuse a term and misdescribe the item, you're likely to have an irate buyer on your hands.

Keeping it brief

> Many items don't need much explanation and a few lines will often suffice.
> Some sellers organise their Item Descriptions by using bullet points, because buyers find this an easy way to absorb a lot of information quickly and that has great merits.
> Written descriptions are much less valuable to mobile buyers, so don't go overboard on items where the snaps, title and Item Specifics do the talking.

PRICE >

Setting the price you want for an item is a delicate balancing act. Obviously you have an idea of the level of price you'd like, but equally you don't want to price yourself out of the market.

You can get a feel for what items similar to yours fetch by checking on eBay itself. Search or browse in the same way as a buyer to find similar items and then keep an eye on them to see how they fare. Another option, as with keywords, is to do a search for Completed Items. This will show you items that have recently ended and the price they sold for. Checking out other sellers and how they do business is perfectly allowable as long as you don't steal their pictures or descriptions.

PAYPAL >

Of course, if you're selling on eBay you need to be able to receive and process the money for your items. Get registered with PayPal before you start – as described in Chapter 3, 'Preparing to sell on eBay' – and it won't take you a moment to add this vital feature to your listing.

This is particularly vital if you sell in a PayPal-only category such as these:

> Computing > Software
> Consumer Electronics > MP3 Players
> Video Games > Consoles
> Wholesale & Job Lots > Mobile & Home Phones
> Business, Office & Industrial > Industrial Supply / MRO

You can offer other payment methods, such as cheque and postal order, but there isn't any real need. PayPal really does rule and apart from a few things (such as cars and pay-on-collection items), it's how you'll receive 99% of your funds. Indeed, for international payments, it's best to accept nothing but PayPal.

POSTAGE >

You also need to state the postage cost of your item up front. For many buyers this is the deciding factor: if your postage charges are too high, you won't get the sale.

In addition, eBay uses postage cost to determine your visibility in search. If you can list an item with a price inclusive of free P&P, so much the better. Using the feature called Fast & Free, where you offer a three-day delivery service that's free to the buyer, bumps you up too.

These services aren't actually free, because you factor them into your overall costs, but it's well worth remembering that offering free postage can make good business sense.

Even if you don't include the postage in the price, to attract buyers you should keep your postal charge as low as possible. After all, if it's a toss-up between your item and a similar one from another seller, this can be the deciding factor.

Within the UK, the Royal Mail and Parcelforce are often the most convenient and cost-effective carriers, although they aren't the only option, as I explain in Chapter 10, 'Saving time and money by being efficient'. It's well worth familiarising yourself with the published rates at:

> http://www.royalmail.com/prices-2013.

Additionally, as most eBayers know, your local post office is able to advise you. Get to know the people there. If you're successful on eBay you will almost certainly be a frequent visitor.

Your other best friend will be your kitchen scales. Once you're armed with the Royal Mail rates you can weigh the items and make a good estimate of the postage costs. Buyers always like to know the price of postage and if you give accurate quotes you will seem like a professional and organised seller. The scales will also ensure that you do not underquote and lose money.

Don't forget to factor the packaging costs into your postage charges. It's vital to ensure that the item you send is packaged well and totally protected. It pays to be inventive with packaging, too. Buyers don't necessarily want expensive wrapping and are happy to receive a parcel that looks amateurish with an intact purchase inside rather than a very smart package that hasn't protected the item at all.

Many sellers recycle old padded envelopes or boxes. Very strong 'envelopes' can be fashioned from cardboard boxes and brown tape. Consider reusing bubble wrap, packing peanuts or other items you receive your purchases in.

As long as the savings you're making are reflected in what the buyer pays, you won't receive any complaints. However, if you charge for new packaging and then recycle, you might have an irate buyer to deal with because they will know you're pocketing the difference. As your eBay business grows in scale, though, you'll inevitably end up buying various forms of packaging rather than being able to recycle.

RETURNS >

By law, people selling as a business must specify a returns policy in line with the Distance Selling Regulations (of which more in

Chapter 23, 'Business essentials'). Even if you aren't selling as a business, detailing what returns you accept makes good sense in the ever more sophisticated world of ecommerce where consumers are more discerning.

As a rule of thumb, the number of returns most sellers get represents no more than a tiny percentage of the dispatches they make. For most, returns are a pain and a hassle, but are not necessarily frequent.

Needless to say, the better the listing is, the less likely a return will be – although sometimes, of course, you'll get a customer you just can't please. Equally, a good returns policy is a huge reassurance to a buyer. It encourages them to buy because it makes them feel safer: they can return the goods if they want to.

There are various aspects of returns that you need to consider.

Knowing the legal requirements

Your returns policy will depend on what you sell and the style of business you run. But as a foundation, find out what you're legally obliged to offer and stick to that. Of course, regardless of whether or not you express your legal requirements, your buyers can enjoy the protection of the law, so make sure you know what that is.

It's a cost of doing business

There's not much point fretting too much about returns. They're an inevitable cost of doing business, whether you're a small-time trader or a high street giant. Some canny sellers specifically budget for returns across all their sales when they calculate their prices (perhaps a little extra on your P&P?), therefore generating a 'returns fund' that covers the sales that go awry.

Being as flexible as you can

It's hard to stress too much how popular returns policies are with buyers. Offering a policy that appeals to the massive number of convenience-oriented shoppers makes sound business sense. By being flexible, you may attract many more buyers and not see a corresponding rise in returns.

6 | Selling your first item

So you've got some stuff to sell and you've decided how you're going to describe it, taken some photos and sorted out all the other aspects of the sale. Now's the time to take the plunge and fill in your very first Sell Your Item form.

Most sellers will confess that they found their first sales very exciting. Waiting for bids and BINs is tantalising and it's a thrill actually to make some money. That said, it's also daunting because it's something new. But if you're serious about making serious money, you have to get started.

LISTING YOUR ITEM >

To list your item on eBay and make it available for people to buy, you need to enter all the content you've already prepared into the Sell Your Item form. This is a series of online pages that allow you to build the View Item page that buyers see. You can get to the Sell Your Item form by clicking on 'Sell' in the Navigation Bar. Make sure that you've already set up and confirmed your Seller Account.

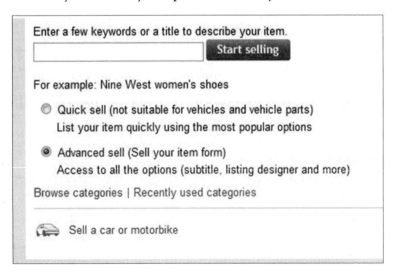

Bear two things in mind when you're filling in the Sell Your Item Form. First, your item isn't available to buyers until you submit the item to the site. You can change, amend and edit the listing as much as you like until it's gone live. Secondly, there's a wealth of information and help on the Sell Your Item form. If you need guidance, the Help pages are just a click away.

Here's the step-by-step process you'll have to go through.

Selecting a category

You will be offered a Search Box and asked to enter relevant keywords related to your item, such as 'Bob the Builder pencil case' or 'Prada purse'.

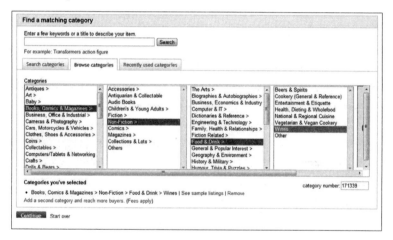

Once you've chosen your category, you're ready to enter the majority of the information: item title, item description and a picture.

Adding a description

Describing your item will be a doddle, because you will already have written your title and item description and have these ready to paste into this page. Simply copy the title from your Word document or similar and paste it into the title space. You can do the same with your description.

You can change the look of your text from within the Sell Your Item form by using the formatting buttons at the top of the Item Description box. Highlight sections or the whole document and change the font, size or colour. You can also alter the alignment of the text and emphasise key details by making them bold, italic or underlined. If you're a computer whizz and have prepared your description using HTML, you need to switch to the HTML tab. If you enter HTML in the normal description field your coding won't work.

To see how your description will look when it's live on the site, click the Preview link near the bottom of the page. You'll also have another opportunity to review the look of your listing on the next page.

There you need to provide some further information, detailed below. Some is compulsory (marked by a green star), some isn't, but make sure that you provide as much information as your buyers will require.

Adding your pictures

If you haven't got a picture ready by the time you reach this stage of the Sell Your Item form, it's a bit late – and a poor use of time – to get your digital camera out and take one now. If you do have one prepared, all you have to do is upload it to eBay. Remember that you have the chance to add four images to each listing for free and it really is a case of the more the merrier.

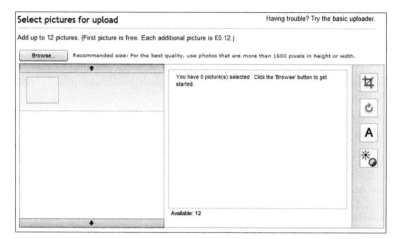

Setting price and format

Now you need to add some of the vital pricing details and how you're selling the item.

You have to choose between the traditional auction format, where buyers bid for your item, and the Buy It Now option, where people don't bid but simply buy your item at the price specified by you. For your first sale, choose the auction format. This way you'll get a real feel for how eBay works. You can experiment with Buy It Now when you've found your eBay feet.

In fact, if this is your first sale you probably won't be able to choose Buy It Now. To use it you need to have five or more unique feedbacks or have given eBay your direct debit details. If you're not qualified to use BIN listings, eBay assumes that you want to sell using an auction and you won't have to take any action.

For an auction, your price needs to be the lowest amount you're willing to settle for if you only get one bid. If you're using BIN, you should specify the price you want.

Deciding duration

You're also required to select how long you want your listing to last for. You have a choice of 1, 3, 5, 7 or 10 days. How long your listing lasts for has no bearing on fees.

Quoting quantity and location

State how many of the item you have to sell and where you and your item(s) are located. No messing about: eBay requires you to be factual.

Putting in post-to locations

Where you're willing to send your item is up to you, but you should be aware that it also determines who can see your listing and the number of potential buyers who can bid. If you choose 'Will Post Worldwide' your item will be available to all eBay members all over the world.

If your item is only going to be attractive to UK buyers, or is too bulky to send overseas, then the 'Will Post to the United Kingdom Only' option will be best for you. You can pick and choose here. If you want to ship to the United States and Canada as well as the UK, or just the UK and Asia, it's totally up to you.

Specifying payment options

You're in the home straight by the time you have to specify your payment and postage preferences. As I've already recommended, you should accept PayPal as an absolute minimum and then any other payment options that suit you. The Sell Your Item form automatically assumes that your PayPal registered email address is the same as the one you've given to eBay. If it isn't, you should add the PayPal email address here. eBay will remember it for future listings.

If you're willing to accept a cheque or other payment through the post, eBay assumes that you want it to be sent to your registered address and tells your buyers that address when the time comes. If you want payment to be sent to a different address, you need to enter that by clicking the 'Change' link under the 'Seller's Payment Address' heading.

It's best to provide a postage cost for UK-based buyers in the relevant field because it saves you time later. If you've followed my advice you'll already have calculated this, and adding it here means a British buyer can make a PayPal payment immediately they've won the item. You can also indicate international postage costs if you like.

> Tip: Make it easy to pay

By entering postage and payment details now, you make it easier for your buyer and yourself. When your listing ends successfully, the buyer automatically receives an email from eBay with all the instructions they need to make their payment. If you don't enter payment details now, you have to email the buyer yourself at the end of the auction.

Adding further info

You will probably need to include some extra details in this section to assist your buyers. For instance, you might want to note that you expect payment within 14 days, that you prefer PayPal or that international bidders should contact you for further details about postage costs. In addition, if you accept returns or offer refunds, this space in the Sell Your Item form is the ideal place to outline your terms.

> Tip: You only enter it once

Much of the information you enter on the Sell Your Item form is common to all your listings. You only need to enter it once and eBay remembers it. When the information has been stored you can make the form easier to navigate by clicking the 'Minimise' button on the right-hand side of the page. When you do this you won't see the options and your stored details will carry on being used until you change them.

OPTIONAL EXTRAS >

The information highlighted so far is the most important for you to specify. Sometimes you might want to make use of the extras on offer on the Sell Your Item form. Most of them have an additional charge attached, but for the right item and seller they can mean better sales. You'll find these on the Create Your Listing page and the one that follows.

Pre-filled item information

Pre-filled Item Information is available if you're selling all sorts of items, but is probably most useful to sellers of books, DVDs and CDs. eBay takes a lot of the grubby work out of listing by providing you with catalogue information. For instance, if you're selling a DVD and you enter the EAN from the barcode on the back of the box, your listing will automatically include details of the film such as the cast, running time, a basic plot description and a stock photograph. For a CD you get the names of the tracks and some notes and reviews.

Obviously this is going to save a bit of time, but it doesn't mean you don't have any work to do. The catalogue information eBay provides for free is just the common information every single item of the same kind has. You still need to include specifics that are only true for your particular item: good and bad. If your item comes complete with extras that others may lack, add those details. If your item has been damaged, then you should note that too, just as you would if you were writing your own description from scratch.

> Tip: Be different
Using Pre-filled Item Information isn't an excuse for being lazy. It will save you a slab of time, but if you really want your listing to work you need to be clever. For instance, because anyone can use Pre-Filled Item Information, the chances are that there will be items that look very similar to yours. In particular, you need to pay attention to the Item Title. If you use the one that's provided, it will be identical to everyone else's. Add to, amend and improve your Item Title so that your listing stands out from the crowd.

Scheduled listing

If you want your item to start, and therefore end, at a particular time but can't be at your computer then, you can choose to schedule your listing. This means you create the listing and send it to eBay immediately, but it won't be available to buyers on the site until the time you specify. The option to schedule a listing costs 12p and you can do so up to three weeks in advance.

Counters

Including a counter is free, so there's no reason not to have one. It shows you how many people have taken a look at your View Item page. This can be a great way of gauging interest and letting you know whether you're attracting people to your listing.

Listing Designer

If you want to give your item a really professional and jazzy look, you can choose a Listing Designer template from the selection eBay has available. This is a graphical border that sets your Item Description off to a tee. Depending on what you're selling, you can choose a theme or colour scheme to complement it. Adding a Listing Designer template costs you an additional 7p, so it can be well worth it if you're selling a high-priced item. Sci-fi fans should check out the 'SpaceCows' theme.

> ### > Inside Information: You can't buy visibility

I'm a sceptic when it comes to paying for listing enhancements to boost your item's visibility on eBay. If you have to, it means something else you're doing is wrong. It could be because your feedback and DSRs aren't up to scratch. In that case, don't spend more money, simply take steps to get better feedback.

Equally, if you haven't fully optimised your listing, it's money wasted. If you could improve your titles, why spend to get more prominence before you have? These features on eBay are predominantly there so the site itself can make a bit more money. Use them sparingly, even experiment a little if you like, but few sellers will make them a central part of their selling strategy.

Private auction

Sometimes people prefer anonymity. If you hold a private auction, no one can see the identities of the bidders. This can be particularly useful if you're selling something very, very unusual (which people might want to be secretive about owning) or something people might be embarrassed to be seen buying. Otherwise, don't use this option. It's free, but it can put off buyers who don't understand the reason for keeping identities hush-hush and are scared away by the cloak-and-dagger approach.

SUBMITTING YOUR LISTING >

Once you get to this point, you're pretty much ready to send your item live to the site and make it available to buyers. This is your opportunity to ensure that the listing you have created is ship-shape and Bristol fashion.

All the information you have submitted is available for your review and you have the opportunity to go back and edit it as you wish by choosing the appropriate link on the left-hand side of the page.

Take a moment to examine the listing fees eBay will be charging you. These are detailed at the bottom of the page and won't be charged until you submit the listing. If you've chosen a feature you don't want to pay for, you can go back and remove it from this page. If you want to include additional features, you can go back and add those too.

When you're happy with your listing, all you need to do is click 'Submit Listing' at the bottom of the page and your item is complete. eBay starts to weave its magic and the item will be added to the Search index and the category you've chosen.

Listing an item really is as easy as that. It may take you some time to get to grips with the Sell form, but practice makes perfect and every time you do it, you get better and faster.

MY eBAY >

Now that you have one or more live listings, you can easily track them using My eBay, which you can access by clicking the 'My eBay' link at the top of most eBay pages and signing in using your User ID and Password. This is an invaluable tool, so learn all about it and you'll get to love it.

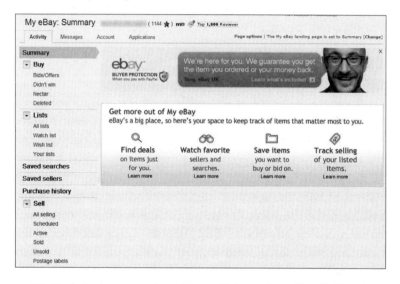

To find the items you're selling, click on the 'All Selling' tab in My eBay and you'll be provided with a list together with a summary of whether your item has bids, the current price and the time the listing ends.

My eBay will also tell you if there is any action you need to take, such as emails that need to be answered or other issues requiring your attention. You can also see how many people are watching your item.

If you want to take a closer look at an item you're selling, simply click on the Item Title in My eBay and you're taken to the View Item page. By clicking 'Bid History' you can see more details about the bidding activity and all the bids you have received. You can also check out the bidders themselves by examining their feedback, as you would with a seller.

To reassure yourself that people really are able to find your listing and are taking the time to check it out, look at the visitor count on the View Item page and see how many visitors you've had. The counter you included in your listing tells you how many people have looked at the item. If they like the look of it and think they might want to place a bid later in the auction, they will add your item to their Watch List. Again, you can see how many watchers you have in My eBay.

MONITORING YOUR ITEMS >

Once your listing is live on eBay and available to buyers, you don't have the luxury of simply sitting back and relaxing until it ends. You still have a little work to do. Taking the time to manage your listing can win you more bids and a better price.

First things first: sit tight and try not to worry. Lots of first-time sellers get anxious when the item they're selling doesn't get any bids in the first few days. Commonly they worry that they've made an error or that buyers can't find the item. This is usually not the case. On eBay, just like at real auctions, bidders prefer to keep their powder dry. Rushing in and placing a bid early on is considered by many to be a surefire way of pushing up the final price.

The vast majority of bids on eBay are placed in the final 24 hours of a listing and often you see the bulk of the bidding going on in the closing minutes. This can make the first days of a listing seem dull for the seller. But just because people aren't bidding, that doesn't mean they aren't looking at your listing and deciding whether it's for them.

Responding to emails
However detailed and full your description is, buyers often contact you directly with questions requiring further information or clarification. The emails are forwarded to your registered email address by eBay. Your email address itself is not disclosed to people who ask you a question. Take the time to answer these

questions honestly and quickly, because that gives a good impression and shows you're a professional seller.

Sometimes you get an email from a member asking you to end the auction early and sell the item to them. They might make you an offer above your asking price if you agree to sell to them there and then. The best advice here is to decline politely. Think about it. If they're willing to pay you £20 for something you've listed for £10, it's possible there are people who are willing to match that offer or even go higher. Also remember that if you agree to sell your item 'off eBay' you won't be eligible for protection or help from eBay if the buyer turns out to be a timewaster — or worse. This is a well-worn tactic that fraudsters use to snare an eBay seller who's a little wet behind the ears. If you accept the off-eBay sale, payment will be made (often by a stolen credit card via PayPal) and you'll send the goods, but a few days later PayPal will reverse the payment. You'll have neither item nor money and you won't be protected by the Seller Protection scheme, because the transaction happened off eBay. Be particularly wary of this kind of scam in electronics categories.

Improving your Item Description

If you receive a question about the item via email, it's possible other people might want to know the same information. You could consider adding the requested information to your listing. If your item has a bid, you can only add information to the View Item page in a separate box. If you don't have any bids, you're free to edit the listing and add or remove anything you want. You can do all this via My eBay.

> Tip: Question and Answer

The Question and Answer feature saves you time and effort. If a potential buyer asks you a question, you can opt to publish the question and your answer on the View Item page. You can do this automatically by selecting the 'Display this question and response on my listing so all buyers can see it' option in the email you receive from eBay.

BEST OFFER AND SECOND CHANCE OFFER >

If you list a fixed-price item, you can invite buyers to make you an offer under the Buy It Now price if you like. Sometimes you get a silly offer that you can't accept, but on other occasions you might be willing to let your item go for a few quid less than it's listed at just to shift it.

You can set rules for Best Offers on the Sell Your Item Form. If you get one above the price you determine, it will be automatically accepted. Otherwise, you can take a call on each one as they come in. They are a good way of generating interest in your item.

If you create an auction listing you can make a Second Chance Offer to your under bidders (unsuccessful bidders) at their highest bid. You can do this in My eBay once the item has ended.

RECEIVING PAYMENT >

If you took a moment to include postage details when you were listing your item, once the auction is over you just need to sit back and wait for the buyer to pay. At the end of the listing they automatically receive an email with the necessary details and you'll find that many buyers simply pay up without any prompting from you. When they complete Checkout, this is noted for you in My eBay and you'll get emails from eBay and PayPal.

Should you have decided not to provide postage details in the listing, eBay will notify you with details of the successful bidder and you'll need to send them the necessary information yourself.

For buyers who pay by PayPal, you receive an email notification with their address so that you can dispatch the item.

If they want to pay by cheque or postal order, you need to wait for the payment to arrive and, if necessary, clear.

CONTACTING THE BUYER >

If the buyer doesn't complete Checkout and you don't hear from them, you need to contact them to make sure everything is OK. Buyers and sellers must contact each other within three days of the listing ending, but a good seller should do it sooner than that and preferably within 24 hours. eBay sends you the buyer's contact details in an email at the end of the listing, and a quick and friendly email to a non-paying buyer usually does the trick.

Sometimes a buyer needs clarification or maybe has a specific request about delivery that you may have to resolve. If they are overseas and you haven't stated a cost for sending the item to their part of the world, you have to provide them with the cost before they can pay you. Sometimes the buyer is new and doesn't know how to complete the purchase, so you need to be patient and helpful as they find their way.

Whenever you're dealing with a buyer, take the time to communicate clearly. They don't know the person behind the User ID, so make sure your emails do you justice. Most misunderstandings and disagreements on eBay, and online generally, are the result of hastily written emails taken the wrong way.

DISPATCHING THE ITEM >

Once your buyer has paid, the ball is in your court: you need to send them the item they have bought. Where possible you should get the item in the post as quickly as you can. Your buyer shouldn't be kept waiting, so the same day or the next one is best. Obviously taking a few days is fine, but if a buyer has to wait any longer than that they often start asking questions.

If you can't dispatch your item within a few days of receiving cleared payment, you should contact the buyer so they know what to expect. Buyers are typically very flexible as long as you keep them informed.

As already noted, it's important to package your item safely and securely. Parcels can get rough treatment as they go through the postal system, so it's best to err on the side of caution when you're judging how well to protect an item. If you're sending your sale overseas, your packaging should be even more robust. If it's going outside the EU you need to fill in and attach a Customs Declaration, which you can get at the post office.

When you do send the item, try to give your parcel the personal touch. Including a pre-printed letter that you've signed is good way of making each and every buyer feel special. Some sellers like to incorporate a handwritten note or card. Any note you do send should thank the buyer for their purchase and encourage them to leave you positive feedback. You should also make sure your buyer is in no doubt that they should contact you if they feel moved to leave negative feedback or a low DSR.

You want to encourage repeat buyers and you want to avoid negative feedback: by making a personal connection and coming across as a caring seller, you can encourage your buyers to think well of you.

LEAVING FEEDBACK FOR YOUR BUYER >

Buyers on eBay can leave positive, negative or neutral feedback. As a seller, you can only leave positive feedback. The decision of when to leave feedback for your buyers is up to you. Many sellers do so when they've received cleared payment.

The thinking behind this view is that once a buyer has paid in good faith, they have fulfilled their obligations. Other sellers disagree and don't leave feedback until they get confirmation that the buyer has received the item and is happy with it.

There are no rules when it comes to leaving feedback for buyers, so you need to decide your own policy. It is true that being the first to leave feedback is a good way of ensuring that your buyer reciprocates. If you want to build your eBay feedback reputation, then it probably makes sense to bite the bullet and leave feedback first.

> Inside Information: Selling surprises

Sometimes when you're selling an item you get a surprise – a good one. If you don't know much about the item you're selling, it could turn out to be worth much more than you imagine.

Two great eBay selling stories stand out as examples. The first is about a seller in America who discovered a beer bottle in his attic. It was old and dusty, but he knew there was a market for collectable breweriana, so he chanced his luck and listed it on eBay, starting the bidding at a dollar.

Little did he know that the bottle he'd found was something of a Holy Grail among collectors. The bidding got off to a good start, but soon the word was out and he was astonished to see bids in the hundreds of dollars. Collectors from all over America were emailing him asking for more details. When the auction ended the seller netted $19,000 for a bottle he might otherwise have thrown away.

A similar story involves a seller who put up a fishing lure or fly on eBay. He didn't know that it was a very rare example from a well-respected maker: it sold for $32,000.

Closer to home there are some fascinating examples of runaway bidding that have amazed sellers. On the UK Discussion Boards there's a member who bought a record at a car boot sale for 5p and sold it on eBay for more than £500. It isn't uncommon to read about sellers who pick up an item for a quid or two and sell it on for £20, £30, £40 or more.

The moral of these stories is twofold. First, they prove the old maxim that one person's junk is another person's treasure. The stuff gathering dust in your loft may well be the one-off collectables that other people spend a lifetime seeking. Second, they demonstrate that if you're going to sell something you don't know much about, eBay is the place. If the sellers of the beer bottle or the fishing fly had been at a car boot sale, they might have raised a few dollars because they didn't know any better. A chuffed collector who couldn't believe their luck would have scuttled off with a smug grin on their face and the bargain of their lives. On eBay, buyers have to battle with each other and when there are lots of bidders who want to buy an item, the seller stands the best chance of getting the price they deserve.

> eBay provides sellers with a selection of tools with the aim of saving them time and encouraging more sales. You shouldn't think of these as advanced, scary or dangerous tools, but instead as quick wins in your search for efficiency. Once you've confidently sold as few as 5 to 10 items, you need to start upgrading and embracing this vital equipment.

TAKING ON TURBO LISTER >

Of all the activities an eBay seller has to do, one of the more irritating is listing items. If you're an ambitious seller it can seem like you can't get the listings up on the site as fast as buyers are snapping your items up. The Sell Your Item form is cumbersome when it comes to listing groups of items one after another, especially when many details in your listings, such as location, payment and postage, are likely to be either the same or very similar for every one you create.

Turbo Lister helps you list more items, more quickly. It's very easy to use, so there's no reason you shouldn't start using it as

soon as you want to begin selling more than two or three items at the same time. It is a very convenient way of organising your selling and is suitable even for low-level sellers. However, it's when you're ramping up the number of listings you're putting on the site that Turbo Lister really comes into its own. If you're used to the Sell Your Item form, trading up to Turbo Lister is like exchanging a Morris Minor for a Boeing 747. It's faster, it's got way more capacity and your sales might actually take off.

Turbo Lister basically offers you flexibility. If you want to list a collection of items on a Saturday night, you don't need to slave over eBay when you'd rather go to the pub. You can create your listings in any spare moment you have during the week and save them on your computer until you want to send them to eBay.

If you have text that you use in all your listings, such as payment and postage information, you can save this in Turbo Lister so it automatically appears in each listing. You can also store your listings templates in Turbo Lister and bulk edit and amend whole batches of items in one go.

Go and download Turbo Lister now. It's free and it will revolutionise your selling. You can load it onto your computer from:
> http://pages.ebay.co.uk/turbo_lister.
It's compatible with Microsoft Windows (although not the Mac operating system) and doesn't require too much disk space.

Using Turbo Lister

When you've downloaded Turbo Lister and installed it on your computer, you need to set up your ID and import your contact details from eBay. You only have to do this once. If you sell using multiple IDs, it's easy to add as many as you like to Turbo Lister and keep your item batches separate.

Once you're up and running, you can make a start on using the tool by creating a new item. You'll see the button in the top left of the Turbo Lister screen.

Unlike on the Sell Your Item form, you don't have to move back and forth from page to page. Every option you need is immediately available and if you want to rationalise the page and get rid of certain functions that you don't use (say you only accept PayPal, in which case you don't need to see all the other options), you can do this.

On the left-hand side is the field where you write your title, add your Item Specifics, attach pictures and tinker with your item description. Like on the Sell Your Item form, you can edit your item description using the Design View or the HTML editor. In fact, everything you can do on the Sell Your Item form you can do in Turbo Lister. On the right-hand side you can enter your price, duration, auction format and payment and postage details.

At the bottom of the page you can see buttons to preview your item, send it to eBay and save the information as a template. This last option is particularly useful if you're selling lots of similar items. Simply create one listing and copy it as many times as you need. You can then merely edit the aspects of each listing that are different, thus saving yourself lots of time. You can also change the appearance of the page using the 'Customise' button.

Once you've created your individual listings, you can store them in Turbo Lister until you want to upload them to eBay, which you do by clicking 'Add to Upload'. You can schedule items in Turbo Lister as you would normally do in Sell Your Item.

Turbo Lister is updated roughly once a month, so get into the habit of making sure you have the latest version. You'll find the update button under the 'Options' tab. Most of the problems you may encounter with Turbo Lister are a result of not updating the program, so it's worth doing this periodically.

Making the most of Turbo Lister

There are lots of natty features in Turbo Lister. In fact, it's rather like a mobile phone: you don't have to use all the functions, but you might be surprised at what it can do if you have a sniff about.

> **Editing in the 'grid'** On the main page of Turbo Lister you'll see a digest of all the items you've created. It's from here that you can keep track of your inventory and make changes as you like. By selecting the items you want to edit, you have the

option to make bulk alterations to your entire inventory. If you want to standardise the returns policy on all your listings, for instance, it won't take you a moment.

> **Search** There's a handy search option, which is particularly useful if you have thousands of items and you need to find a particular listing quickly.

> **Importing and exporting active or ended items** If you have items that have run their course on eBay and you want to keep the details to use again in future listings, you can easily export the details to Turbo Lister for recycling.

> **Importing and exporting with CSV** If you like to keep the details of your listings in a spreadsheet (such as Excel), you can easily plug Turbo Lister into your own system. By using the CSV format you can import and export your listing details quickly.

UPGRADING TO SELLING MANAGER OR SELLING MANAGER PRO >

When you start off on eBay as a seller, you manage and monitor your listings via the selling tab in My eBay. There you can see how your sales are progressing and also perform tasks like leaving feedback at the click of a button. But as you've no doubt been discovering, as you increase your sales you need different and more powerful tools that recognise the changing scale of your activities and sales.

eBay offers two customisable options to sellers who are making more than a handful of sales. Think of them as beefed-up equivalents of My eBay honed to the needs of sophisticated users. They both reside in My eBay and when you upgrade, they simply replace the Sell tab. These tools are called Selling Manager and Selling Manager Pro and each has different options and services that are of use depending on your experience. Upgrading is definitely going to save you time and effort as you expand your sales.

Bear in mind that both Selling Manager and Selling Manager Pro are management tools rather than listings tools. If you're looking for a service that helps you list more quickly and easily, then they won't really help you. That's what Turbo Lister's for.

Selling Manager

The less sophisticated of the two tools is Selling Manager. It's free to subscribe to and offers some great time-saving features. There really isn't a reason not to get started with Selling Manager because it's free and useful. It's also very much like My eBay, so you shouldn't find it too tricky to get used to.

Selling Manager offers you all the functions that My eBay provides, which means you won't lose anything by upgrading. You can use it to manage all your current, past and pending listings and in addition enjoy some extra features:

> **Sending emails** Every seller has to deal with a large number of emails. Whether it's informing buyers that they've won, chasing payments or telling customers that their item has been dispatched, it's not unusual to be sending two or three emails per transaction, if not more. Multiply that by the number of items you sell and you're sending hundreds if not thousands of emails a week. Anything you can do to be more efficient here is therefore good news. With Selling Manager you can automatically generate emails with pre-populated details about the items that you've sold. eBay provides you with templates, but you can produce your own to ensure you get your desired message across.
> **Bulk relisting** Relisting unsold items one by one can be a time-consuming and dull experience. It's also highly inefficient. In Selling Manager you can relist in bulk: you simply tick the items you want to relist, click one button and away you go.
> **Printing labels and invoices** Selling Manager is hooked up with PayPal. You can use it to print out invoices for your buyers or address labels for your parcels. Once you've got this function set up, you may find it a great way to claim back some minutes every day. The templates available from eBay also make your packages look smart and professional.

> **Storing feedback comments**   As a seller you probably find yourself leaving the same feedback comments again and again. It may only take a moment to do one, but when you look over the course of a month you might be leaving hundreds of feedback comments and the time adds up. In Selling Manager you can store up to 10 customised feedback messages that you can then use as appropriate.

Selling Manager Pro

Selling Manager Pro has all the functions of Selling Manager plus some very neat extras. It costs £4.99 a month, which some people baulk at, but it's best to think of it in terms of the time you save. Even if you can claim back an hour a week by upgrading, it's a bargain.

> **Sending bulk emails**   In Selling Manager, as I've explained, you can write and create your own standard emails to send out to buyers. In Selling Manager Pro, you can send out these emails in bulk. So if you need to send 10 emails telling 10 buyers that their item's been dispatched, you can select them from your list of sold items by ticking a box and sending them all an email at once. This can save you a whole lot of time.
> **Automating emails**   Not only can you create reusable templates for emails, you can choose to automate when they're sent, so you can dispatch personalised emails to buyers automatically when they pay, for instance. This is a great way of coming across as a very diligent seller when in fact you might not be anywhere near a computer at the time the email arrives.
> **Automating feedback**   Leaving feedback is one of those jobs that you just have to do, day in, day out, and it can be repetitive and dull. With Selling Manager Pro you can automate feedback to be left when a buyer performs a particular action. For instance, you can automate your feedback to be left the moment someone pays with PayPal, or you can program feedback to be left only after the buyer has left you a positive remark.

> **Reporting** Selling Manager Pro can be a source of some interesting and useful numbers and reports that can help you understand your activities. You can use it to calculate profit and loss as well examine your conversion rates (how many of your listed items actually sell) and average selling prices.
> **Managing inventory** If you're selling lots of identical items, it's worth checking out the inventory management tools in Selling Manager Pro. If you've got 100 widgets and you sell 100 on eBay, when you try and sell widget 101, the program lets you know that you're out of stock.
> **Managing inventory templates** You might frequently be selling the same items and using similar or identical listings. In Selling Manager Pro you can download listings you've already created from the Sell Your Item form or Turbo Lister and update them as required.

TERAPEAK >

Wouldn't it be useful if you could not only examine what you're doing yourself but also compare that to other sellers, and then also draw conclusions by benchmarking that information to the eBay marketplace as a whole? You can. Step forward a commercial (off-eBay) market research service called Terapeak.

It's difficult to emphasise how useful and powerful this tool is. It allows you to get a full health check of your business against a background of other sellers on eBay. It costs $30 a month and sometimes people tell me that they can't justify the expense, but I just shake my head and say, 'If you're serious about making money, you can't afford not to use it.'

Terapeak has two key benefits. The first comes when you're sourcing stock. When you're in negotiations with a supplier, it allows you to see how similar lines have fared on eBay in the past 90 days. You can find out prices, conversion rates and whether demand is waning or not. This is immensely valuable information if you're just about to shell out a load of money on new inventory.

Secondly, you can monitor your performance. Are you doing as well as other sellers in your categories? All the data comes direct from eBay, so it's totally accurate, and you can realistically chart your position in the marketplace.

Terapeak is valuable and vital for serious sellers. Check it out:

> http://www.terapeak.com/

> There's a ton of stuff you need to know about eBay. In this handy chapter I've gathered together some of the most frequently asked questions that baffle fledgling eBayers. Sometimes there isn't an easy answer and a lot will depend on what you sell and the nature of your business, but my answers should give you some idea.

WHAT ARE eBAY'S SELLING RULES AND POLICIES? >

eBay has a complex selection of rules that even the most expert of eBay sellers will never know inside out. These rules fall into roughly two categories: rules about things you can't sell; and rules about how you sell. First, restricted items. This is just a digest: spend a bit of time checking out the items you can't sell on the eBay website:

> http://pages.ebay.co.uk/help/policies/index.html

Most of these items are banned for obvious reasons. You can't sell guns, knives, bootlegged and pirated media, drugs, pornography, human body parts, animals, plants or alcohol (unless the bottle or container is collectable in its own right and is more sought after than the contents). eBay prohibits 'hate items' too, such as those related to the Nazis, the KKK and serial killers.

How does eBay know if I'm selling prohibited or restricted items?

eBay has a very effective policing system in place: all the other buyers and sellers. If a member sees a restricted item for sale, there's a strong chance they will report it to eBay. For some sellers this is a great way to eliminate competition, but for others it's simply a way of keeping eBay safe. Needless to say, eBay also has all manner of monitors and filters running in the background to detect infringing items.

What does eBay do if it finds out I'm selling restricted items?

eBay takes a very dim view of sellers who break the rules. If you do list an item that's prohibited or restricted and it's your first offence, eBay will probably merely end the item, refund your fees and give you a warning. If you continue to break the rules, however, you will be suspended and banned from the site. Depending on the severity of the offence, a ban may be temporary or permanent. So disregarding the rules is a big business risk.

WHAT ARE eBAY'S LISTING POLICIES? >

When it comes to how you sell, most of the policies are straightforward and make perfect sense, although some are complex. This section is only a summary of the most important ones. For full details of the listing policies, which are updated occasionally, visit:

> http://pages.ebay.co.uk/help/policies/listing-ov.html

Links

There is a strict policy governing the links you can include in your listing. You are not allowed to have links to other websites unless they are credits or links for payment services, photographs or further details about the item for sale.

Surcharges

It is normal practice for sellers to pass on postage and handling costs to their buyer. However, these must be reasonable and stated up front where possible. You may not pass on the cost of taking online payments when using a service such as PayPal. If you're processing credit card payments using your own merchant service, you are permitted to charge a surcharge to cover your costs.

Keyword spamming

As mentioned earlier, you're not allowed to include irrelevant words in your Item Title so that it gets more attention from the search facility. For instance, if you're selling a Swatch watch you're not permitted to list it as 'Swatch not Rolex' so that more people find it when searching.

Fee avoidance

Obviously eBay isn't keen on any feature of a listing that means the seller is avoiding its selling fees. You're not allowed to list an item with a very low price and high postage so you can avoid fees but not lose money. You're also not allowed to list an item for a low price but say in the listing that the price will in fact be much higher.

WHAT ARE eBAY'S SELLING FEES? >

eBay's selling fees can seem complicated to newcomers. In fact they're a bit of a mystery to old-timers too: they get changed frequently and with each change a further level of complexity is added. But don't let this put you off.

Understanding eBay's fees is critical to being a profitable and effective eBay seller. Different features and enhancements on eBay incur different fees. I recommend you check out the full and official list of fees at:

> http://pages.ebay.co.uk/help/sell/fees.html

> Inside Information: Fees

It's a fairly obvious point to make, but nevertheless: you want to keep your eBay fees as low as possible. While that's easier than it sounds, keeping a close eye on what you're paying is time and money well spent for every eBay seller.

What's the average level of fees paid by eBay sellers? It's impossible to say. But I'll stick my neck out and say that if you're paying more than 20%, you probably have room for savings. The biggest scope for savings lies with listing fees. You particularly want to be cutting back on incurring fees that don't result in a sale.

Listing fees

These are the fees you pay to put an item on eBay. They vary depending on the category, your reputation as a seller, the value of the item you're selling and the starting price you've chosen.

> ### > Tip: Category-specific listing fees
> If you sell technology goods such as phones, computing gear, consumer electronics and photographic supplies, or media items like CDs, DVDs and books, comics or magazines, you're eligible for a different fee structure, honed to make sales in those categories more affordable. Find it at:
> > http://pages.ebay.co.uk/help/sell/fees.html

Final Value Fee

This is the commission you pay when an item sells. Again, it varies depending on the value of the item that sells and the category it sold in.

Feature fees

If you want your items to stand out, you can pay extra fees to enhance your listing with features such as a subtitle.

Subscriptions

Some services on eBay attract subs, such as an eBay shop or using Selling Manager Pro. If it's an additional service, the chances are there'll be a fee.

> ### > Tip: Fee savings
> The biggest opportunity for saving on eBay fees is by benefiting from the preferential listing fees offered to shop owners. The subs on an eBay shop justify these reductions alone.

WHEN ARE THE TAX AUTHORITIES INTERESTED? >

Information on business registration and tax returns is examined in greater detail later on in the book, but a simple rule of thumb applies to dealing with the tax man. If you start buying things to sell, then you'll need to start keeping records for your tax return and began accounting for tax on your profits.

Of course, when you start doing business as a trader you also need to inform the authorities within about 100 days of commencement. That paperwork isn't tricky and will be looked at in detail in Chapter 23, 'Business essentials'.

What is also clear is that the tax authorities have been keeping a greater eye on eBay of late and are interested in pursuing people who dodge their tax responsibilities. In 2012 they sent out over 100,000 letters to eBay traders asking them to come clean. Remember, eBay is a very open marketplace and it's not hard to tot up someone's sales from their publicly available feedback page.

HOW DO I CONTACT eBAY? >

Getting the hang of using eBay's own help systems before you start selling is a very good idea. This way, when you need to find out something in a hurry later, you'll be able to keep your swearing to a minimum.

Customer support on eBay

On the Navigation Bar at the top of nearly every eBay page you can see a link to 'Customer Support'. This gives you access to eBay's dedicated Help pages. There are hundreds and hundreds of pages containing information and advice on all aspects of trading on the site. Whether you want to know about selling pet food, advice on setting a safe password or information about payment methods, you may find what you want here.

What if I can't find the information I want?

With so much information available and so many questions you might want answered, it's possible that you won't be able to find the answer or that it might not even be included in the Help pages. If you can't find the information you require, you will need to contact Customer Support or try out the Community Help Boards. To get in touch with the customer support staff, there's a Contact eBay link on the Customer Support hub.

> ### > Inside Information: eBay customer support
> eBay doesn't have a very good reputation in providing direct customer support. Ask most eBayers and they'll tell you that it's often difficult to get the answer you want quickly and the response you will receive will be a stock reply.
>
> To be honest, you're best off trying to get your own answers and to do that you should get to know eBay's Help section. Other eBayers are also a great source of expertise, so asking your question on the Discussion Boards is often your best hope.

> ### > Tip: Use Google
> You might find it easier to use Google to get help in relation to eBay, as it has a better search facility than the eBay Help pages. Start your search with 'eBay UK Help' followed by what you want to find out about.

CAN THE COMMUNITY HELP? >

eBay provides Discussion Boards so that community members can discuss their trading, meet friends and enjoy themselves. All registered members can use the Discussion Boards and they offer a unique opportunity to contact other buyers and sellers.

Sometimes the best person to get help from is someone who understands exactly what you're experiencing. You can find these people on the Discussion Boards. eBay can give general advice about communicating with a seller or filing an alert for a buyer who hasn't coughed up, but if you want first-hand experience from other sellers and buyers, the best people to ask are those who might have faced the same issue before. Other eBay members can give you personal insights and candid responses.

Many eBay members take a real pride in offering help to less experienced traders. They are very keen to give quick and factual replies about all aspects of eBay trading as well as tips and hints. Think of the Discussion Boards as the place to go to get insider knowledge.

You can find the Discussion Boards by clicking 'Community' on the Navigation Bar and following the link to the Discussion Boards. There are numerous discussion boards for all sorts of trading topics.

HOW DO I FIND THE eBAY ANSWER CENTRE? >

If the Discussion Boards are too scary for you, try the Answer Centre, which is a more structured and ordered way of getting help from other members. You can get there by clicking on 'Community' in the Navigation Bar and selecting the 'Answer Centre' link halfway down the page.

In the Answer Centre you'll see a selection of topics related to eBay buying and selling. Pick the one that's most appropriate for you and check out the questions asked and the answers given. If your question isn't addressed, then just ask it yourself and wait for replies from other members. You usually find you get your answer pretty quickly.

WHERE DOES eBAY MAKE ANNOUNCEMENTS? >

One important way in which eBay communicates with buyers and sellers is via the Announcement Board. Think of this as its official noticeboard for members. If there's a change in a policy or an enhancement to the website on its way, eBay puts it on the Announcement Board. Also, if there's been a problem with the website, eBay will often note it here and inform members of any refunds that are due. The Announcement Board on eBay.co.uk publishes information specific to UK traders.

The Announcement Board is regularly updated and the more you use eBay the more invaluable the information will become. You can also see a digest of recent announcements on the Summary page of My eBay.

In addition, the System Status Board should be your first stop if there's an issue or problem with the site. Inevitably with a website the size of eBay, with so many different functions and features, problems do sometimes occur. If there is an outage or problem eBay will record it on the System Status Board.

You can access both of these boards by clicking on the Community link in the Navigation Bar.

WHERE CAN I FIND HELP ON PAYPAL? >

Just like eBay, PayPal has a comprehensive Help section for you to refer to if you get stuck. You can access it by going to the PayPal homepage: www.paypal.co.uk.

In the top right-hand corner you will see a text link to 'Help'. Click on it and you will be taken to the Help Centre. You have three ways to find the information you want. PayPal lists the questions most people ask on this page, so the chances are that a simple query might be addressed there. If it isn't, check out the categories on the left-hand side and navigate down to the topic you want. You can also search PayPal's Help resources using the

Search Box on this page, in the same way as you'd search eBay's Help.

You can contact PayPal's Customer Support team via this page by clicking the 'Contact Us' link on the left-hand side, at the bottom of the list of categories. You can also contact PayPal via email or telephone during business hours at the national rate.

An eBay shop is an off-the-peg, instant ecommerce presence that you can personalise and use to reflect your own type of sales and eBay persona. Opening a shop not only provides you with lots of useful tools and features to help you sell even more successfully, but sends a message to your buyers that you're an advanced seller. Typically a shop owner sells 25% more than a seller without a shop, so there are lots of benefits here for the serious money-making eBayer.

An eBay shop also comes with a host of perks: you can get your hands on a clutch of free listings, a stack of fee reductions and also a selection of features that justify the costs in themselves.

According to eBay, 75% of eBay sellers who have a shop say it has helped them increase sales. It seems fair to assume that the other 25% haven't built their shop correctly or have failed to utilise its functions to best effect. A well-constructed shop is sure to give you a boost in your sales.

The good news is that you don't need to be a computer whizz or know HTML to build a shop. You can customise your shop from a selection of options and you're guided through the

process by the eBay Shop Builder. You can personalise the shop with a logo and your selected colour scheme and also organise how your items are displayed in a matter of minutes.

THE BENEFITS OF AN eBAY SHOP >

An eBay shop sits on the eBay site and people can easily navigate to it via Search and Browse, but it can also act as though it's a standalone entity. The shop comes complete with your own URL (web address) that you can use as you wish on business cards or other promotional material to direct buyers straight there.

You have control over the shop design and how you organise your items. This means that whether you're selling dozens of things or thousands, you can build your own category structure just like on the eBay site to help buyers navigate your wares quickly and easily. Visit the eBay Shops homepage at http://stores.ebay.co.uk and check out a range of shops that have been opened by other sellers.

Furthermore, Chris Dawson of Tamebay.com is quick to point out that the benefits of an eBay Shop lie primarily in the preferential fees a seller can get when they subscribe.

'The first and most important reason for having an eBay shop is quite simply eBay fees,' says Chris. 'eBay charge an insertion fee each time you list a product on their site, and for fixed-price listings you can reduce this from 40p per listing down to 10p, 5p or even list for free depending on what sort of level shop you have.

'In addition, if you list overseas you can access free fixed-price insertion fees in Europe and Australia as well as reduced fees when selling on eBay.com. Aside from pure financial benefits, having an eBay shop gives buyers somewhere to browse your merchandise, you set the buyer experience including your own categories instead of eBay's defaults for how your products are displayed and which items are promoted, and of course you can market to your previous buyers with eBay shop email marketing and use Markdown Manager to drive revenues by holding a sale.'

The full benefits of an eBay shop are tweaked and amended quite often (usually for the better), so keep an eye on what's on offer at the page that lists the benefits:

> http://ebay.co.uk/storefronts/subscriptions.html

COSTS >

A Basic Shop represents excellent value at £14.99 per month. If you want to take your shop selling to the next level, you might want to upgrade. For £49.99 a month you can have a Featured Shop, which offers some enhancements and also much greater prominence on eBay and more attractive fee reductions.

For £349.99 a month you can have an Anchor Shop. It's an expense for sure, but it attracts increased fee reductions and additional international visibility that mean you can develop your overseas trade. You just need to do the sums to work out whether you'll make a saving. Those listing fees do add up when you're a serious seller and an Anchor Shop can save you much more than it costs.

SETTING UP SHOP >

Getting your shop up and running shouldn't take you more than an hour or so. First, examine what other sellers are doing and how they are using their shops. You'll doubtless get some excellent ideas from them and gain a good grasp of the functionality on offer.

There are five constituent parts you need to consider in relation to an eBay shop and it's best if you prepare them in advance. You need to choose a shop name, select a design, describe your shop and what you're selling, and also build your categories. In addition, although this won't be visible on your shop front, you have to enter keywords designed for the search engine spiders.

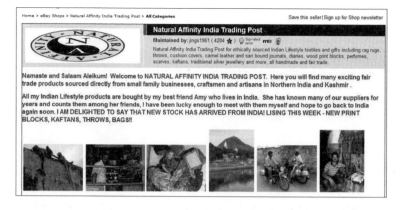

Home > eBay Shops > Natural Affinity India Trading Post > **All Categories**   Save this seller | Sign up for Shop newsletter

Natural Affinity India Trading Post

Maintained by: jings1961 (4204 ☆)

Natural Affinity India Trading Post for ethically sourced Indian Lifestyle textiles and gifts including rag rugs, throws, cushion covers, camel leather and san bound journals, diaries, wood print blocks, perfumes, scarves, kaftans, traditional silver jewellery and more, all handmade and fair trade.

Namaste and Salaam Aleikum! Welcome to NATURAL AFFINITY INDIA TRADING POST. Here you will find many exciting fair trade products sourced directly from small family businesses, craftsmen and artisans in Northern India and Kashmir.

All my Indian Lifestyle products are bought by my best friend Amy who lives in India. She has known many of our suppliers for years and counts them among her friends, I have been lucky enough to meet with them myself and hope to go back to India again soon. I AM DELIGHTED TO SAY THAT NEW STOCK HAS ARRIVED FROM INDIA! LISING THIS WEEK - NEW PRINT BLOCKS, KAFTANS, THROWS, BAGS!!

Choosing a name

You already have an eBay User ID and you can use that for your shop name if you like, but it pays to be more adventurous to ensure that you reap the full rewards. Much like item titles, with a bit of thought you can really squeeze extra value from your shop name. It's obvious from shop names you see on eBay that most sellers aren't aware of the huge dividend a perfect choice could bring them; don't make the same mistake.

The temptation is to name your shop something cute or personal – 'Dan's Den', for instance – but this might not be the best way to attract buyers. The name of your shop is critical to its appearance in search engines, particularly as good visibility means you can also attract buyers from outside eBay. Search engines pay great attention to the shop name, so you benefit from choosing one that searchers will pick up. While people aren't going to search for 'Dan's Den', a shop called 'Bargain Books and DVDs' will be found by those searching for just that.

Selecting a design

You can easily decide on a colour scheme and layout using eBay's free templates and designs. This won't take long and it gives you an opportunity to personalise your shop. eBay has made a selection available, but it's best to create your own for that really personal touch. In fact, when you build your shop it's an excellent opportunity to review the branding and design of all your

listings, including getting a logo designed if you don't already have one.

Use consistent colours and fonts across all your eBay pages. The aim is to ensure that your buyers know they are shopping with you and that they notice if they leave your pages.

Customising your shop design

Your eBay Shop is completely customisable and many bigger sellers want something that looks more professional and exciting than the free, basic templates provided through the design wizard. If you have HTML and design skills you can create a great shop yourself, or companies exist who will do the design and coding for you.

If you're interested, check out Frooition (www.frooition.com) or Just Template It (www.justtemplateit.com).

Describing your shop

You also need to write a shop description and create your custom categories. Again, these are important for making your shop attractive to search engines. The spiders pay attention to words or phrases that are repeated on a page, so make sure your categories and description reflect what you sell as well as your shop name.

Here's an example of a shop description:

> My name is Dan and welcome to my shop. I take pride in selling lovely old books that I have collected over the years and also DVDs. Thanks for stopping by!

That might be friendly and personal, but this would be much better:

> Buy books and DVDs. Paperback books, Hardback books, Fiction, Non-Fiction, First Editions, New and Secondhand, DVDs, Thrillers, Comedy, Drama.

Obviously your description will be relevant to what you're selling, but be aware that using the specialist terms your buyers are familiar with is best. You should include brand names and alternative terms too whenever possible.

Designing your shop categories

When you decide on your category structure you should have two aims in mind: cramming in as many keywords as possible and making it easy for buyers to find what they want. This is your opportunity to craft a navigation system that is honed to suit your sales and your buyers, so you want relevant, descriptive terms that reflect what people actually search for.

Entering keywords

The final stage requires you to enter keywords for each of your shop pages and categories. The keywords you use when you're setting up shop are of great importance to search engines, but their power is only completely unleashed if you've chosen an effective title, optimised your categories and crafted a really good shop description.

You can find the fields to enter your keywords under the heading 'Keywords' in the left-hand navigation pane of your shop management console. All you have to do is enter the keywords that are relevant to your shop. eBay will help you make the right choices and then conceal them in the code of your site, where search engines can find them and use them to catalogue and index your shop correctly.

GETTING THE MOST FROM YOUR SHOP >

Once your shop is up and running and you've got some categories and some listings within it, there are some extra things you can do to make your venture even more successful.

Shop header

Your shop header is a graphic that sits on your listings directing people straight to your shop. It contains your shop logo and name, and you can also include a selection of your shop categories so buyers can get straight to the items they want. The shop header is a vital way of building your brand and putting your sales right in front of browsers and buyers. Take a look at how other sellers are using the header and think about how you can design it to maximise sales, as well as adding it to all your listings.

Cross-promotion options

At the bottom of many listings you see boxes displaying other items that seller has for sale, which is known as cross-promotion. As a shop seller you have lots of options related to which of your items are cross-promoted and how they are displayed and prioritised.

Depending on what you want to sell, you can opt to display the most expensive items, the cheapest or those without bids. You can set your cross-promotion preferences and your shops header in My eBay via the link 'Seller, Manage Shop'.

Promotional boxes

It's possible to create promotional boxes for your shop that you can position on your homepage to draw attention to special sales.

You have total flexibility in titling the promotional box and you can link directly to one of your items or perhaps one of your shop categories. You can also use these boxes to give buyers the chance to view your shop items in your preferred order. For instance, on the main eBay site many buyers are attracted by search and browse listings set to a Gallery view, with the items ending soonest shown first. You could use a promotional box to do the same in your shop.

Custom pages

One way of really personalising your shop is to create pages of your own. You have great flexibility in what you can do and a quick browse on eBay will show the variety of ways shop owners use this kind of customisation. It's a great means of setting out all your policies and telling buyers why you're a great seller. And there's also a business benefit to creating these pages: they get picked up by the search engines.

Markdown Manager

Everyone loves the buzz of the sales and the thrill of finding a bargain. But to get your buyers salivating, they need to know how much they're saving. The Markdown Manager is a tool available to shop sellers that shows buyers how much the item they're looking at has been discounted. Sellers can choose when items are discounted and by how much, even determining this in advance. Don't worry, it isn't permanent: you're completely in control and can change and edit your reductions at any time.

Mailing lists and email marketing

Email marketing is a powerful way of reaching out to other eBayers and encouraging repeat sales. You aren't permitted to send out unsolicited emails to all and sundry, but you can invite browsers and buyers to join your mailing list, then send emails advertising your wares to those who have opted in. Encourage people to join your mailing list by advertising it in your listings, shop header and all the emails you send out when people buy items.

You can organise the people who opt in by adding them to particular lists depending on what they've bought from you in the past. That makes it easier to reach out to them with targeted email marketing. To build and send a marketing email, click 'Email Marketing' in your shops management console.

Shops reporting

Of all the functions you get with an eBay shop, one of the most important is the traffic and sales reporting features. From what I've heard from the shop owners I've met, it's also one of the most overlooked.

The traffic reports tell you how many visitors you've had to your items and your shop. You can find out which of your pages is the most visited, which of your listings is getting the highest number of hits and which keywords buyers are using to find your listings, which means you won't leave out the most important ones in your Item Descriptions.

Traffic reporting is a great way of understanding what's working and what's not. For instance, if that seven-day auction format listing that you start at 8pm on a Tuesday is getting three times more visits than the ten-day one you started on a Thursday at noon, you might want to ditch the next Thursday listing or start it at 8pm instead.

> Getting the basics of selling on eBay right is the foundation of your campaign to make serious money. But once you've mastered those everyday tasks of sourcing, listing, selling and dispatching your goods to happy punters, you need to become more ambitious. You have to face the challenge of innovation.

That means doing things better, smarter, cheaper and more quickly. It's a relentless battle to keep up and improve, but being more efficient and effective must be baked into your daily routine.

Part of being efficient is making more time to develop your enterprise even further. Striding forth and embracing change are part and parcel of the ecommerce challenge – they are also what make it fun. Outwitting the competition, whizzing ahead of the crowd and just being jolly clever are immensely satisfying and will reward you with profits as well.

BUILDING AN EFFICIENT OPERATION >

Tools such as Turbo Lister, Selling Manager and Selling Manager Pro will save you bags of time. But it's by improving the way you work and creating a robust and efficient back end for your operations that you discover the most scope and opportunity to improve your efficiency and ramp up sales more quickly, particularly as a business seller.

You need to unleash your inner Henry Ford and examine the tasks you do every day to understand what's taking up your time, what can be done more swiftly and what can be done away with altogether. However you look at it, your time is your most valuable resource, so you don't want to waste it. On one level it might be galling to work out the 'hourly rate' you're earning from your eBay sales and discover that it's pitifully small, but that can be a useful wake-up call, reminding you your productivity isn't what it could be.

To boost your earnings per hour, you need to be more efficient. And if you want to develop your business and eBay activities, you need to find time to invest in them. You might also just want more time to spend with family and friends.

That's what improving your efficiency means: doing more in less time. Only you can take ownership of your time. Some of the tips listed below will work for you, some of them won't, but there's something here for everyone. I haven't yet met an eBay seller (and I've met thousands) who can't benefit from at least one of these suggestions.

To give you an idea of what you might gain, consider the car parts seller who reorganised his whole warehouse. He developed a system of stations based on the stages of an eBay sale: one station for photography, one for listing, one for packing, one for dispatching and so on. He employed a number of people, so being as efficient as possible really was about saving money. He examined his new system and discovered that he was about 20% more efficient. That's like getting another day in the working week for free.

BATCHING UP TASKS >

Think about it: taking ten photos doesn't take ten times as long as taking one – not when you take into account the time you spend getting the camera out, preparing an uncluttered space to form the background, firing up the image software and realising that your batteries have run out. Batch up other similar tasks too, such as writing descriptions, packaging, replying to emails and crafting listings, and do them all in one go.

Apply a production line mentality and tackle each task in turn. When you research your categories, for instance, it's easier to decide on all of them while you're in the relevant part of the eBay site. With Turbo Lister or using the scheduling function, it makes no odds when you create the listing or in what order you gather together its various components. Print out your dispatch notes once a day and 'pick and pack' once a day too. You could even consider packaging items in advance, rather than 'on demand' when they've sold.

OPTIMISING YOUR WORKSPACE >

First up, if you possibly can, have a workspace dedicated to your eBay selling. It can be anywhere from a whole room to the corner of a table, just as long as it's got everything you need easily to hand. It would drive me mad to have to dash to the kitchen to get the tape or the scissors, the cupboard under the stairs for a padded bag, the desk for a print-out and the bottom of the wardrobe for the item itself. Those kinds of shenanigans are a monumental waste of time.

I went to see a seller once who was in the throes of getting her dispatches ready for the day. She was complaining she never had enough time to list more items, she could just about keep up with the ones she was doing and eBay needed to be easier and quicker to use. As she was ranting, I must have looked rather like a tennis umpire: she was flitting from one end of the room to the other, from her desk to the printer, grabbing dispatch printouts one at a time. She wasn't amused when I suggested she might save a bit of time if she moved the printer next to her computer.

Analyse the tasks you need to do and how they can be done most efficiently, then form your working space around that process as best you can. Aim to create an eBay production line.

LETTING YOUR LISTINGS DO THE WORK >

If you're getting lots of emails during sales, or find yourself chasing buyers for payment, responding to queries about combined shipping or dealing with non-payers, you need to optimise your View Item pages. Make sure that your listings are doing as much of your work as possible.

Are there changes you could make to ensure that people don't have to come to you for an answer? If there are, make the change once and eliminate the need to do it time and time again. Don't forget the FAQ facility that you can insert into the Ask Seller a Question process.

BULKING UP AND AUTOMATING >

Are you really getting the most out of the tools eBay offers to make you more efficient? The automated email systems in Selling Manager and Selling Manager Pro can be an absolute godsend. Automated feedback is a boon too. You could also save time by using the function that allows you to bulk print your invoices, or change one single aspect across all of your listings with the bulk edit tool.

It really is worth familiarising yourself with these various programs to see what you're not using or checking what's been added since you last looked. eBay is often improving and developing the tools with little fanfare or explanation.

Consider whether other services might also be useful. Many companies offer handy eBay tools (alas, often with a charge) that might be just what you need. Ask fellow sellers or have a look on Google.

POST HASTE >

If there's one thing eBay sellers sink more time into than anything else, it's posting and dispatching their items. From weighing and assessing the cost of postage, to queues at the post office or dealing with the fallout from a Royal Mail snafu, it all takes time. Here are some aspects to think about:

> You can print out postage labels without going anywhere near a Post Office. Check this out at:
> > http://www.royalmail.com/personal/uk-delivery/online-postage

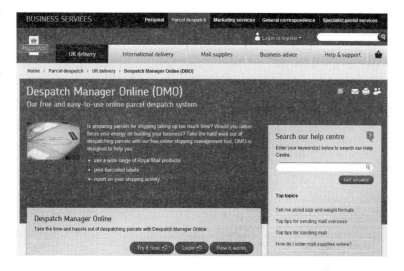

> Fill in your paperwork at home. Get a stash of the forms you're going to need from the Post Office and complete them before you leave.
> If you're sending out lots of parcels, look at getting the Royal Mail to come by and collect them. It may not be as expensive as you think and if you're sending out a serious number of parcels (a yearly spend at the Post Office of £15,000 or more), you won't get charged at all for this service. Again, costs and how to set up an account can be found at:
>   > http://www.royalmail.com/general-correspondence/ uk-delivery/printed-postage-impression-ppis
> Talk to the staff at your Post Office. If you're spending a lot of time there, see if they can help you. When are their quiet, queue-free times? I've even heard of some accommodating branches that open early or late to deal with valuable, regular eBay customers.

CATCHING ON TO COURIERS >

In addition, the once dominant behemoth of the Royal Mail is no longer the default choice for online sellers who are selling in volume. Especially if you're selling something bulky or heavy within the UK, it won't be the best option for you. There's a huge selection of new and nimble courier services yapping at its heels and you'd do well to be aware of them.

Courier services have pros and cons. First, they don't usually offer a universal service. Surcharges may well apply if you're sending gear to Scotland or Northern Ireland. They also may not be as swift as the normal post, but then as long as a buyer knows a service is going to take 3–5 days they'll be happy with that if the price is right.

Here are four services you could usefully check out:

> MyHermes   https://www.myhermes.co.uk
> Collect+   http://www.collectplus.co.uk
> Parcel2Go   http://www.parcel2go.com
> DespatchBay   http://despatchbay.com

For further options, check out the Tamebay Guide:
   > http://tamebayguide.com/shipping

HAVING THE RIGHT TOOLS >

Is your kit fit for purpose? As mentioned before, simple improvements to your gear and equipment could free up time. A faster, more reliable printer might be a very sound investment. Fed up with struggling with brown tape? Buy a tape gun! And always ensure you have enough of the right packaging to hand.

Consider your computer too. Broadband is essential, is now available just about everywhere in the UK and is getting cheaper. Also check that your computer is running as fast as it can. Don't forget there are often preferential allowances available to businesses when upgrading computer equipment courtesy of the Chancellor of the Exchequer.

EMBEDDING RECORD KEEPING IN YOUR PROCESSES >

No one likes doing the paperwork, but it has to be done neverthe-less. Make sure a problem isn't looming over you by understand-ing what records you need to keep for what reasons and doing them as you go along.

The most efficient sellers I've seen at work have paperwork seamlessly embedded in their daily routines. It's certainly better than staying up all night with a shoebox full of receipts and the self-assessment tax deadline fast approaching.

IT'S LESS BOVVER WITHOUT A HOVER >

How much time do you spend 'just checking' your listings? How many times a day do you find yourself 'having a quick look' at your emails? How much of this is strictly necessary? There are very few emails that can't wait a few hours for a response. Of course a swift reply is good practice, but it doesn't have to be immediate. You certainly don't need to remain hunched over your inbox waiting for emails to arrive. Dealing with emails in one go at dedicated times each day makes much more sense.

In the same vein, hovering over My eBay obsessing over your latest Buy It Nows and bids is not time well spent. Limit your checking to certain points each day and try sating your (admi-rable) curiosity with your reports. Understanding which of your keywords is driving the most traffic and sales is more valuable than knowing that at 18.41 you got a new watcher on item X.

KICKING THE BAD HABITS >

Are you always leaving your daily packaging too late? Is every trip to the post office a last-minute dash before it shuts? Are you con-stantly running out of padded bags? Do you consistently create your listings late at night? Every eBay seller has a bad habit that they could eliminate in order to become more efficient. You know what yours is – work out how to kick it.

PLANNING AND SETTING DEADLINES >

Making plans, setting deadlines and creating lists of what you need to do by when are invaluable ways of making sure you're achieving what you want. Without a boss keeping an eye on you, it can sometimes be difficult to motivate yourself to get down to the daily tasks or to look to the longer term and create a strategy for maintaining your business. An informal list of objectives or a short quarterly plan, in addition to your immediate to-do list, is good business practice.

TRADING SAFELY AS A BUSINESS >

Just because you're now a serious seller, it doesn't mean you can forget about safety. As a business you're potentially at greater risk from the fraudsters, so you mustn't let your guard down.

All the same threats remain as for personal sellers and you need to make sure you're protected. Obviously there's the eBay Safety Centre as a source of information, but do check out Get Safe Online, which has a dedicated section for businesses. It's your indispensable guide to what you need to know:

> www.getsafeonline

Case study | The trading assistant | eBay User ID: stuffusell
http://www.stuffusell.co.uk

Stuffusell doesn't actually sell anything of its own: it's a sort of broker. It sells for other people. That can be big businesses liquidating stock, fire sales or selling on behalf of individuals who maybe don't have the time or expertise to sell for themselves.

The business is the brainchild of David Brackin. He came to eBay with a degree in Maths from Cambridge, a solid business background in management consultancy and a desire to exploit what he saw as an opportunity.

When I visited his west London warehouse, the place was crammed full of stuff that was for sale (or waiting to be listed), and it was organised to be efficient. His team have special stations for taking images, listing the items and then making sure they get everything out of the door to couriers and carriers as quickly as possible once they're bought and paid for.

The success of his business is down to reputation, according to David. He keeps a keen and daily eye on his feedback and DSRs and knows that even a handful of bad reviews could be harmful.

'For our clients, it's not just about knowing how to use eBay or saving time,' says David, 'but research shows that as a result of our reputation, size, experience and pricing know-how we get higher prices in the marketplace than casual sellers. Many of our best clients are experienced eBay sellers who recognise the value in having someone else deal with the logistical and communications hassles. Furthermore, the service is anonymous so celebrities and others can sell without fear of negative publicity.'

Of course, services like David's don't come cheap – 35% of the sale price plus VAT – but the uplift in prices that a good reputation on eBay gets you can often exceed the cost of sale. Obviously the buyers contribute to the postage charges. So far the business has sold gear on eBay worth in excess of £7 million.

Chapter 6, 'Selling your first item', looked at how you can create a basic listing that engages a buyer and encourages them to bid on your item. But when you're trying to make dozens of sales and build your turnover and profitability, you have to work harder at crafting your listings. This won't be as big a chore now as it was when you were an eBay newbie, because your experience and knowledge will be greater. Nevertheless, 'making do' isn't an option any more. You need to look slick, professional and competent in order to stand out from the army of other sellers.

eBay is a competitive marketplace and the Darwinian principle of 'survival of the fittest' really does apply when it comes to buyers selecting sellers from whom to buy. eBay offers you many ways to differentiate yourself from the horde. Obviously price is one key area (some people like to buy the cheapest item available regardless of any other considerations) and feedback is important too. But there are other ways in which you can compete and your greatest opportunity to differentiate yourself from the competition is by crafting superior listings.

In fact, if your listings are compelling enough you can even compete effectively with sellers who are selling the same items for less than you are, because your listings will be more attractive and will thus generate greater trust.

Think about this in terms of displaying items for sale in the offline world. At a car boot sale it's perfectly acceptable to lay a sheet on the floor and put the items you're selling out on that. On the high street you generally see something more sophisticated, although even those displays vary from a basic line-up of products (like you'd see in a local shoe shop) to the extravagant works of presentation art in somewhere like Selfridges.

Displaying your items correctly, finding as many customers as possible and engaging them sufficiently to persuade them to get their wallets out is the name of the game. It's also about saying as much as you can about yourself by implicitly reassuring buyers that you're the best seller to buy from. Crafting the perfect listing and maximising its effect and impact will make sure that you get the best return on your listing fee investment. Here are some suggestions.

THE TITLE IS VITAL >

When you're building the perfect eBay listing, the most important aspect is the Item Title. This is the number one tool that every seller has to attract buyers in the marketplace, yet many sellers spend little time and effort honing it. Titles are something almost everyone is failing to maximise.

Why is the Item Title so important? It's how buyers find what you're selling – it really is as simple as that. Everything follows from the Item Title. You can have perfect pictures, a compelling item description, correct categorisation, rock-bottom postage and a superb price that buyers will love, but if people can't find and view the listing you have lovingly crafted, then you have, quite frankly, wasted your time and your listing fee.

You can even pay eBay extra fees for glitzy features like Bold and Highlight and it won't make the slightest difference. When it comes to getting the buyers in, you need to make sure that your Item Title is working as hard as it possibly can for you and your sales. To do that, you need to understand how eBay works and how your buyers think.

What is an Item Title?

On the most basic level, an Item Title is the name of the listing you are building. But actually it's much more than that. It's easy to fall into the trap that catches the vast majority of sellers: they think they have a very clear view of what an Item Title is and that's what they enter. Often a seller says to me 'It describes what I'm selling' or 'It's how I would search for what I'm selling'.

The problem is that an Item Title isn't about describing an item at all and it doesn't matter for a second what the seller searches for (because a seller is selling products, not buying them). An Item Title is not a headline and it's not a way of cataloguing something. It's actually how you match your item to a buyer who's looking for it. Simple, huh?

Think about it: is attracting buyers your primary motive when you write your title? Or do you just type in the first words that come into your head? I think every seller on eBay can improve their Item Titles, and they can do it by discarding their own views and embracing those of the people who want to buy something.

Only 80 characters

Your Item Title is limited to 80 characters, which isn't a lot. You need to be brutal and scientific in your choice of words to get the most out of it, particularly by removing irrelevant or redundant terms or unnecessary punctuation.

Many people think that the subtitle and the item description are also searchable on eBay (and they are), but the default search is Item Title only and the vast majority of people on eBay don't change that setting. You need to base your thinking on the assumption that people are only going to search for the Item Title.

You also need to think about 'browsers': people who don't search eBay using keywords. They browse through the category structure, starting with the long list on the left-hand side. They may start with 'Home and Garden' and then narrow down their search until they find your antique lamp, without ever putting 'antique lamp' into the search engine. Roughly 25% of eBay buyers browse, so you also need to make sure that your Item Titles make at least some sense to those who find them by looking through the relevant categories.

But my Item Titles work already!

I'm sure they do. I bet people find your items and I bet those who find them think the Item Titles you use are great. But what about people who are looking for what you're selling and haven't found you? You haven't constructed an Item Title that works for them. If you want to succeed on eBay you're going to have to hook those people too.

You can attract new buyers simply by making small changes. Here's a great example. An eBayer I know sells women's fashion. She was doing very well using Item Titles that described exactly what she was selling. She was including sizes, details of designers and great information about the fabrics and quality of her clothes that was accurate and useful. In fact, she didn't think there was anything wrong at all: she was happy with the amount of stock she was shifting. But the trade she was doing was a fraction of the potential sales available – her Item Titles weren't doing the job for a great many of the people who were searching for her type of product on eBay.

Once she'd done a bit of research (in the ways I describe in a minute) she found that some of the most commonly used search terms relating to what she was selling were not included in her Item Titles. When she did include those terms, in the first week alone her sales were up 30%. After a few months she dramatically expanded her operations and took on two staff – business is booming.

What are people searching for?

The key to constructing a winning Item Title is making sure that it aligns, as closely as possible, to what the people who want to buy your item are searching for. But how do you know that? There are a number of resources available to all sellers and most of them are free.

Obviously, the first thing you want to do is figure out what's working: the words in your Item Titles that are already bringing the bidders in. You can find this out anecdotally or by using the reports that eBay makes available. First up, ask your customers the keywords they used to find your item. Don't forget that you, as a specialist, might use very different words to describe your products in comparison to a layperson. Potential buyers might also be searching for your items but thinking about them in a very different way to you as the seller.

When it comes to a mobile phone, for instance, make and model might not necessarily be uppermost in a buyer's mind.

Some people will simply be looking for a phone they can use with a particular service provider, or one with a good camera, and other buyers might be swayed by the phone's colour. By doing some research, for example by browsing through Completed Items to discover which keywords other sellers are using, you can work out how best to optimise your Item Titles to appeal to the broadest possible audience.

Traffic reports

If you have an eBay shop, one of the best benefits is the free traffic report. In many ways this report is worth the shop subscription alone, because you should easily be able to get your money's worth by optimising your sales.

The report you're looking for is 'Top keywords that drove traffic to your Store', because it shows exactly which keywords people used to get to your shop and your listings. In the first instance this information tells you what's working already and what you shouldn't be ditching from your Item Titles.

It also tells you what isn't working. If you have a keyword in your Item Titles that isn't driving traffic, or not much, then you might want to consider dropping it in favour of a more useful one. Many sellers like to include their shop name or User ID in their Item Titles, for instance; while this might bring in a few customers, it's not likely to be a significant driver. You can use the traffic report to validate your own hunches and your informal customer research, but if in doubt, trust the numbers. You may not agree that a certain search term is the right one, and your customers might have given you different ideas, but if the data says that something works, trust the data.

You can access the traffic reports from My eBay. On the left-hand side you'll see the link 'Manage my Shop'. Click on that and on the Shops Management page, again on the left-hand side, you'll see a link to 'Traffic Reports'. Click on that and sign in to access the reports.

A word about keyword spamming

Keyword spamming is when you add a keyword to your Item Title that's popular with searchers but isn't relevant to the item you're selling. It could be as easy as adding an irrelevant term (for instance if you're selling Adidas trainers, adding Nike) or saying that something is like or not like something else (stating 'Adidas not Nike' or 'Adidas like Nike', for example).

When it comes to keyword spamming, don't do it. Not only is it against eBay rules and you risk being sanctioned, but it also doesn't really work. After all, if people are looking for one thing and you present them with another, it's not a great experience.

Keyword spamming is one of those things that dodgy sellers do, so it could actually cost you sales.

Your Item Titles checklist

> Find out what's working by talking to your customers.
> Find out what's not working by using the research tools.
> Remove needless words and punctuation to create more space.
> Optimise your Item Titles by experimenting with new keywords.
> Review your Item Titles from time to time and optimise them again if necessary.

IMPROVING YOUR WRITTEN DESCRIPTION >

The other critical aspect of your listing that can be tweaked to improve your selling success is the Item Description. Unlike with the title, where the secret is cramming in as much as you potentially can, optimising your description is about taking things out.

Be as descriptive and helpful as you absolutely can be in as short and succinct a way as possible. How your page is structured is also important: lead your buyer through the item in a reassuring and helpful way.

Ditch the blurb. Some sellers really put off buyers by including long, commanding and forbidding rules in their listings: 'I won't do this' or 'You have to do this' and 'I don't accept that'.

In many cases this makes the seller look somewhat misanthropic and unpleasant. Where possible, cut out the extraneous details or confine them to a page other than your View Item page.

> ### Inside Information: Invest in HTML
HTML – HyperText Markup Language – may look slightly pointless and rather dull, but you'd be wrong. A basic understanding of how the language works is something that will serve you well on eBay and on the web more generally. I'm not suggesting complete fluency, just a few key phrases, rather like when you go on holiday. It's nice to be able to say please and thank-you and hello and goodbye in the native tongue, even if anything else leaves you lost.

It's also worth learning the HTML tags for hosting an image and creating a hyperlink. Get your hands on a cheap manual or check out some of the online tutorials on YouTube, which have details of all the tags you will ever need. I can't promise you'll have a fun-filled time getting to grips with HTML, but it will certainly be effort well spent.

GAMING BEST MATCH >

As I mentioned earlier, the system that eBay uses to display search results to buyers is called 'Best Match'. It's reasonably complex and eBay doesn't make it entirely clear exactly how the system works. But we do know a few things for sure.

First, a seller's feedback DSRs are important. If they start to slip, you'll soon find that your prominence in search will be diminished. The only solution there is to work on upping those DSRs by dramatically improving the service you provide. As ever, the best tonic for flagging DSRs is to underpromise and over-deliver in order to wow buyers with an amazing service that's better than they expect.

The other factor that affects Best Match is past sales on particular listings. This is where the importance of eBay's 30-day multiple fixed-price listings come in. If a listing makes a sale, eBay considers it to be more important and will present it more frequently to buyers in search. This makes it vital to get sales on an item early on, so that for the rest of the duration of the listing, it will enjoy greater buoyancy.

Here are some ideas to help you with Best Match.

Just being the best

The best listings will always win. Simply think (again) about amazing titles, perfect pictures and engaging descriptions.

If you have an eBay shop, promote new listings using cross-promotion and via other marketing channels such as email. If you make an early sale you'll reap the benefit for the next 30 days.

Relisting successful listings

If one of your listings is very successful, make sure you relist the item if you can so it can continue to perform strongly.

Offering free P&P

eBay loves sellers who offer free P&P and promotes relevant listings on the site. Make use of this additional profile and let it lead to sales to boost your Best Match performance.

Keeping on experimenting

We don't have a definitive notion of exactly how Best Match works, so experiment with timings and improving your listings, and monitor whether your changes have a positive impact on how you appear in search. You may be pleasantly surprised.

VALUING VIDEOS >

You don't have to stick to static images in your listings. As you're ramping up your sales you might want to consider including videos. It's surprising that more sellers don't do this. Videos are

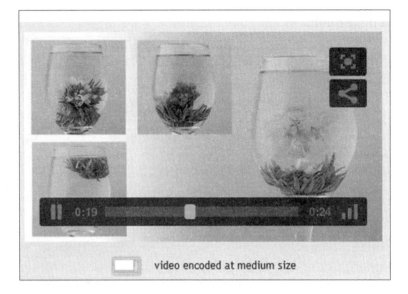

video encoded at medium size

a superb way of showing off your products and they're seen so rarely on eBay that they still have a real impact on buyers.

For instance, on a listing selling remote control cars the seller had incorporated a captivating video of tricks and stunts. If you might be in a position to benefit from videos of your products, the option is really worth looking at.

eBay doesn't offer the opportunity to host videos so you need to find a hosting service yourself, but this shouldn't pose too much of a problem. Services such as YouTube (youtube.com), Vimeo (vimeo.com) and Revver (revver.com) are well known and offer a good service, for free. The real benefit of using a site like YouTube is that you can make the videos available on the site and also link back to your eBay listings, making your videos an advert for your sales.

Another option is vzaar (vzaar.com), a UK-based enterprise founded by former eBay staff. It plugs into eBay's API, meaning your vzaar-hosted videos can be directly inserted into your eBay listings without too much fuss. There are free and paid-for options depending on how many videos you want to upload.

Making a video

Making a moving digital image is pretty easy. Many phones and digital cameras have video capabilities, so if you don't mind a slightly scratchy film quality that will do the trick very nicely. To be fair, the better the camera, the better the video, so some of your results could be very good indeed. For top-notch videos a digital video camera is what you need. Although they are still quite pricey, they enable you to create videos with a wow factor. Most photo-editing programs also have video-editing capabilities, so you can use these to polish your videos to the full.

OTHER USEFUL TOOLS >

Over the past few years, as eBay has grown and sellers have needed more and more help to get the most out of the marketplace, a thriving ecosystem of tools and services has developed.

While most of them attract a charge, investing in something that will save you time and money is good business sense. Here are just a handful that illustrate the range of tools you can bag and the problems they can help you solve. If you want to get a handle on the huge wealth of tools available, check out the Tamebay Guide:

> http://tamebayguide.com/

Accounting

Dealing with your finances is boring but vital and is often a big sink of time in any seller's calendar. You'll be most efficient if you can get your accounting process integrated with your sales data and automated as best you can. Two services in particular are getting great reviews from sellers I meet. Tradebox is provided by Sage and optimised for online traders:

> http://www.tradebox.uk.com/

or you can have a go with Freeagent:

> http://www.freeagent.com/

Remove the Background

This company, based in Denmark, offers such a nifty little service that I have to include it. It makes your photos even more handy by removing all the background in the image so the buyer can focus on the item for sale. If you're reusing images a lot, the charge for this service, starting at 59p a pop, is excellent value and a good way to stand out from the crowd. Moreover, these pics look great on eBay's mobile apps and Amazon too:

> http://www.removethebackground.co.uk/

Translation

International trading is ever more vital and a great way to grow your business. The language barrier is not always a problem, but by making sales available in the native tongue of overseas buyers, you can boost your turnover.

Night classes are no longer essential, as help is at hand. One of the companies that specialise in this area is Webinterpret, which can help not just with your listings but in smoothing out the bumps with overseas selling.

> http://www.webinterpret.com/

Chartixx

It's good seller discipline to understand your sales and the numbers that lie beneath them. Chartixx offers a useful service so you can run bespoke reports on your sales results and how you might improve them. The good news is that the company offers a 15-day free trial.

> http://www.chartixx.com/

Frooition

This UK-based company has a great reputation for creating good-looking eBay shops and also helping sellers jazz up their listings with design and improved usability, leading to better conversion and sales. But one further thing that caught my eye are the Froo Apps, little tools and features that you can drop into your listings to add interest to buyers and showcase your full inventory.

> http://apps.froo.com/

Case study | GMDC Global

John Pemberton manages GMDC Global Ltd, a company that sells on eBay using three different shops: give_me_designer_clothes, designer-clothes-2u and premium_designer_clothes. John also sells on Amazon and is working on his own webshop, www.designerclothes2u. com. He sells suits, jackets, coats, trousers, shoes and accessories from over 500 world-famous designer brands, including Dr Martens.

John is typical of the new breed of eBay seller. He identified the eBay opportunity and proactively decided to build a business rather than stumbling into ecommerce accidentally. Early on he realised that selling online is massively different from running a high street shop. 'Online you have to present the item and convince a customer it is right for them without them touching or trying it on for size,' he says. 'One thing I offer that many shops don't is detailed measurements and in-depth information about an item.'

John has been operating his business for nearly ten years. He broke even at the end of year one and has been profitable ever since. He has consistently grown and developed his sales and describes his business as the number one menswear seller on eBay UK. However, it hasn't always been easy. 'Running and growing a business is a challenge,' John told me, 'and it takes resilience. As time goes on, profits grow, and the nature of obstacles changes.'

John is sticking with eBay because it's a well-established marketplace and he still sees room for growth there, but he's also looking elsewhere. Amazon was his first stop: 'Amazon is a wonderful marketplace, innovative and technically well constructed. As a buyer I find it uncomplicated, clutter-free and easy to buy on.' His move to Amazon is about finding new customers and sales in addition to eBay, not as a replacement. Amazon is also harder to use from a seller's point of view, John says.

What's the secret of successfully starting an ecommerce business? John is clear: 'For me it's a simple thing – success is being able to sell lots of product for a net profit in the least time possible, while achieving a high customer satisfaction rating.' He makes it sound so straightforward.

12 | Troubleshooting

Sometimes things fall apart. eBay is complex and there are all manner of problems and challenges that are sent to test even the most assiduous and honest seller. This chapter considers a selection of suggestions and solutions for dealing with the most commonly occurring bogeymen that test a seller's patience. One aspect is identical across all these situations, though: keep your cool. There's nothing that can't be overcome by a calm and inventive head.

ITEMS THAT AREN'T SELLING WELL >

If you're concerned that your goods aren't selling very well, there are three possible problems:

> There's something wrong with what you're peddling.
> There's something wrong with how you're selling the item.
> There's something not quite right with you as a seller.

Let's take each issue in turn.

To ascertain whether it's your stock that's the problem, it's a good idea to check out how other people who are selling the same stuff are getting on. You might think this information is hidden or unavailable, but it isn't. To benchmark your performance against that of other sellers in the marketplace you can use Terapeak, which I looked at in Chapter 7, 'Managing your eBay sales'.

Terapeak is licensed directly by eBay to provide marketplace data, so it's completely legit. Using Terapeak you can identify different items and different sellers to measure your performance against. With a particular sprocket you might be selling, you can see what recent selling prices have been for other sellers and the marketplace in general. If no one's doing any better than you are, then the goods aren't up to snuff and you should be selling something else.

If other sellers are doing fine with similar stock, then you have several courses of action. The first is to review the quality of your listings. Chapter 11, 'Maximising your listings', addresses some of the things you can do to make yours perfect.

Or is it you that's the problem? It could be that your eBay profile and feedback/DSRs aren't good enough yet and people can't find you. One way to remedy that is to have some loss leaders and special sales that exist purely to boost the reviews you're getting from buyers. This is by no means a long-term solution and you don't want to be spending too much money on it, but a few weeks bolstering your feedback can be well worth the effort. In fact, in your earliest days as a trader it's a good idea in any case. Think of it as an investment of time and money in your future on eBay.

TRICKY BUYERS AND THE eBAY DISPUTE SYSTEM >

At some point you'll inevitably have to deal with a tricky customer on eBay. However, this is also a useful test of your mettle as a seller and businessperson. Often your choices will be limited: as a professional trader you're bound by law to offer refunds and take returns in certain situations, so bone up on the law to find out about your obligations. (There's more in Chapter 23, 'Business essentials'.)

The big mistake is taking any problems personally. If you screwed up, apologise. If you didn't and the buyer is trying it on, treat them courteously and professionally. Even irritating buyers have consumer rights.

The worst possible thing you can do is get into a battle, although this frequently does happen. Maybe the seller is adamant that they're in the right and the buyer thinks not. What follows is an escalating volley of shrill emails and mud slinging that can sometimes last for days or even weeks.

Let's be clear. In most cases where you have a dispute with the buyer, you will be arguing essentially over the matter of a few pounds. Get that into perspective. Wasting time and emotional energy on something like that, even to the point where it dominates your week, is clearly ludicrous. Let it go so you can concentrate on more important things.

Also be careful of your reputation with eBay: it keeps track of the disputes you have with buyers and it will remove Top-rated Seller status from someone who has upset too many buyers. So when a buyer raises a dispute, don't raise your hackles. Resolve it amicably and swiftly and move on.

> Inside Information: Dealing with difficult buyers

I've said it before and I'll say it again: the vast majority of people on eBay are good and honest. But some are less than perfect and can be difficult to deal with. You have to summon up a bit of patience when someone like this turns up.

The most frequent annoying eBayer is the one who buys but doesn't pay. Obviously you can get your Final Value Fee back, but it's also a pain to chase the buyer and file a dispute. Of the hundreds of sales I have had on eBay I can put my hand on my heart and say that not more than four or five buyers have failed to pay.

The most irritating was an American who just couldn't seem to understand that I was located in Britain, that we don't use the dollar over here and that postage from the UK to the US was rather more than from Utah to Oregon. He refused to pay because he was convinced I was trying to fleece him. It was frustrating, but thankfully unique in my eBay experience. I prefer to recall the dozens of pleasant and successful trades I've done with our chums in the US.

Then there are people who are just difficult to please. I had one buyer – whom I eventually refunded when he sent me the item back – who was adamant that the item I dispatched wasn't the one I'd listed because it looked slightly different in real life to the photograph on eBay. Needless to say, it was one and the same item. One buyer sent me a snotty email after he received a 78rpm record he'd bought from me, complaining that he was surprised the item had arrived in one piece considering the quality of the packaging. His item had arrived intact and in one piece (as did all the others I sent out), but he simply wanted to have a go.

PAYPAL LIMITS AND PROBLEMS >

There are two PayPal problems that can happen out of the blue as you start selling on eBay and they can cause genuine annoyance. Alas, there isn't much you can do but be aware of them.

The first concern is the PayPal selling limit. Needless to say, PayPal is required by the authorities to monitor its users for the rare instances of behaviour that might be indicative of money laundering or might be terrorism related. The corollary of this is that it means there are some systems in place that everyday sellers are prone to fall foul of. The first comes when you've been trading a while and you've taken lots of money through your PayPal account. All of a sudden, PayPal freezes the account and asks for verification of your identity and other details.

When this happens, get on the phone to PayPal, find out what it needs and then provide it. It could be a photocopied bill showing your address or a copy of your passport. The company is just verifying your identity and if you're on the ball this problem can be resolved in a few days.

PayPal also looks for odd behaviour in sellers, so if you normally sell low-value widgets and suddenly start listing high-value tech items, it will get a bit suspicious. The buyer may have paid, but PayPal will freeze the funds until the recipient leaves positive feedback or 21 days elapse without a problem. It's a pain in the backside for sure, but it's just one of those things you will have to live with if it happens to you.

DEALING WITH BAD FEEDBACK >

This is a situation you just have to live with. eBay will seldom – once in a blue moon – remove or amend bad feedback or DSRs, but it's not something you should bank on. If you do receive bad feedback, the best advice is to stay calm and keep selling.

DEALING WITH UNPAID ITEMS >

Every now and again a buyer doesn't pay. This is an unfortunate fact of eBay life, but it's by no means a typical experience. eBay recognises that transactions go awry for all sorts of reasons. Some buyers have a legitimate, if annoying, reason for backing out, while others are simply timewasters. The Unpaid Item process means you can claim back your Final Value Fee for an item that hasn't been paid for. It also alerts eBay that a buyer might be unreliable.

Filing an Unpaid Item Dispute

You can file an Unpaid Item Dispute up to 45 days after the listing has ended. Sometimes you know quite quickly if a buyer isn't going to pay: they might tell you they've made a mistake in their bid or that they can't actually afford the item. In these circumstances you can file a dispute immediately.

If the buyer's from overseas and says they've sent you payment in the post, you shouldn't expect to wait more than 30 days for payment. Even if you think their payment is on the way, it may be worth filing a dispute just to be on the safe side. Filing a dispute doesn't mean you have to follow it through: if the buyer pays up you can retract it.

Attempting to resolve the dispute

The next step in the process is to communicate with the buyer and attempt to resolve the situation. The ideal resolution is for the buyer to pay up and fulfil their obligation. When you file your dispute the buyer gets an email reminding them to contact you and pay up. Even if they don't want to pay, they're encouraged to contact you and explain why. Many buyers do cough up at this point and all is well.

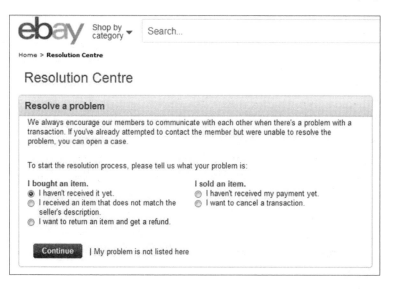

Getting your Final Value Fee back

If your buyer responds and you're unable to resolve the issue, or you don't hear back from them after seven days, you can close the dispute and get your Final Value Fee back. Details of the disputes you have filed are listed in My eBay so you can keep track of them.

Why bother?

Even if you are only claiming a few pence from eBay when a buyer backs out, it's still worth filing an Unpaid Item Dispute, because it helps eBay keep an eye on unreliable buyers. If a buyer gets three strikes for non-payment, they will most probably be suspended from the site unless there are significant mitigating circumstances. By claiming back your few pence you are helping other sellers.

Minimising unpaid items

There is a useful feature on eBay that can help minimise non-paying bidders: Immediate Payments. On the Sell Your Item form you can choose to require a buyer to pay immediately via PayPal if they win your item. When they bid they have to enter their PayPal details, so payment can be taken if they win. This is a good option if you don't want to risk a non-paying bidder, although it does mean people who don't have PayPal accounts can't buy your item.

You can find out full details here:

> http://pages.ebay.co.uk/help/sell/unpaid-items.html

HOW TO CANCEL A BID AND
BLOCK OR REPORT A BUYER >

As the seller, you are free to cancel bids for whatever reason you choose. If you don't like a bidder's feedback, you're within your rights to cancel their bid. The bidder is then free to bid again, so it's polite to inform them that you have cancelled their bid and why.

Don't forget that a bidder with no feedback isn't necessarily a bad person: it wasn't so long ago that you had no feedback yourself. Usually a friendly email to a zero-rated bidder assuages your fears that they aren't bidding in bad faith. You can block all buyers who have –1 feedback or less if you like. You can also ban any buyer who's had a non-payment strike in the last month or who isn't located in a country you're willing to send your item to. Another option is to insist on your bidders being registered PayPal members. You can change your preferences in My eBay using the 'Buyer Management' link.

Cancelling bids only removes the bids from one item. In some extreme instances you might want to block a bidder from bidding on any of your items ever again, and in that case you can add them to your Blocked Bidder list. This bidder will no longer be able to bid on any of your sales until you remove them from the list. You can add any member to the list regardless of whether they've bid on any of your items or not. You can cancel bids and add members to your Blocked Bidder list via My eBay.

There's also a way to alert eBay to a nefarious buyer who might be a repeat troublemaker of general annoyance. On the right-hand side of every View Item Page, there's a Report a Buyer link. Here's hoping you don't need to use it too often.

Case study | The scientific approach | Website: madcowbeads.com

Georgina Davies is unusual as an eBay seller because she's started from scratch and ramped up her business not once but twice and expects to do so again in the future. In 2005 she was successfully selling in the equestrian supplies category and she had an offer to buy the business she'd established. She took the chance and used it as an opportunity to think about what she was going to do next with eBay. 'I had several ideas for future projects,' she told me. 'But I decided to rest awhile and travel around the world. So, we sold our house, stored our belongings, lodged the cats with a friend (who I met through eBay!) and set off overseas for the trip of a lifetime.'

She returned with a clear idea of what she wanted to do: 'My other hobby was making jewellery, so the next move was obvious. I like to stick to what I know, as I think this helps me understand my customers well.' She didn't launch straight in to her new venture but rather took the time to research and plan, and she advises other sellers to do the same. 'Researching and preparing first will really help you get off to a flying start. Plan, plan, plan and plan some more. Set some goals before you start.'

Her advice for sellers who are embarking on eBay is simple: 'Do lots of test purchases. Which experiences made you go "Wow" and why? What problems did you have? How can you make sure that your business delivers consistent customer delight? It's exceptionally competitive in all categories on eBay and "OK" doesn't cut it any more.

'You may get away with it once, but the customer who thought you were "OK" is far less likely to return to you. Without a good level of returning customers you will find business growth far harder.' She also advises against simplifying buyers' motivations. 'Price is very rarely the only motivator. Please don't think that all your customer wants is "cheapest".' She reckons you can make more of an impact and more sales with good customer service. 'I truly believe that the lack of customer focus and drive is very much the weakness of many eBay businesses.'

For Georgie, eBay lets her live the life she wants without the stress of a corporate career. 'As an individual, eBay offers me exceptional flexibility and a quality of life I had not experienced up to now. To succeed in style, rather than just scrape along, you need to work very hard, but the upside is you can plan your workload and sort out your work/life balance permanently. In fact I don't even regard it as work.'

She has already started from scratch twice and she plans to do it again: 'I am very good at setting up systems and businesses and moving them on from start-ups to solid small businesses. I intend to keep spotting niches and filling them, building up a website or printed catalogue and then selling the business on.'

13 | Selling to international buyers

> Roughly 15 million Britons visit eBay each month and the site's total global membership exceeds 300 million. By limiting yourself to domestic sales only, you're seriously reducing your potential customer base. It's time to go global.

THE INTERNATIONAL PRIZE >

Selling internationally is something you need to incorporate into your selling mindset as you build your eBay business. There are very, very few sellers who can't do a bit of international trading. Of course, some sales come to you from overseas without your having to canvass for them, but to maximise the sales you make you need to add specific information to your listings. The first step is to indicate which countries you're willing to ship to on the Sell Your Item form or in Turbo Lister.

Why are buyers from overseas so attractive? First, as is obvious, there are quite simply more people abroad than here at home. Think about it. By opening up your sales to just the EU and North America, you will have a market of somewhere close to ten times more potential customers than in Britain alone.

Secondly, ecommerce is growing faster in other countries. While it would be inaccurate to characterise British, European and American ecommerce as mature, growth is slowing. The big boom has gone, ecommerce is expanding only gently and customers are becoming more demanding. However, elsewhere in the world ecommerce is continuing to boom.

We're talking BRICs and CIVETS here, the world's big and upcoming economies. The BRICs are Brazil, Russia, India and China. Those four countries represent about a third of the human race (around 2.5 billion out of a total of 7 billion) and they are getting involved in ecommerce at a pace.

The CIVETS are the next league down: Colombia, Indonesia, Vietnam, Egypt, Turkey and South Africa. All of these countries are developing at a dizzying speed, want Western convenience ASAP and are soon to become much bigger players on the international stage.

Third, and most important, international buyers are often your most valuable customers. Our chums across the water will often pay premium prices for British goods because they quite simply can't get them in their own country. That means order values tend to be higher and you're likely to sell multiple items in a single sale. It's also one of those occasions when it's great to be British. Lots of folk around the world love British goods and brands and want to get their hands on what we make.

> Tip: eBay shops help international trade
One of the big perks of an eBay shop is the free access it gives to international markets. eBay actually charges extra fees if you want your listings to appear on the bigger sites such as eBay.com and eBay.au. When you have a shop, these fees are dramatically increased, making it a sound investment if you sell overseas.

MAXIMISING OVERSEAS SALES >

The key is to make it as easy for your international buyers to buy from you as it is for domestic buyers by giving them the information they need to take the plunge. The simple fact is that selling internationally can mean a bit more work and hassle for you, but if you get it right, international sales could easily become a significant chunk of your business.

Postage
Research postage costs in advance. If you can determine the costs for the UK, then you can use the internet to work them

out for just about anywhere in the world. You should wise up to the different deals for international carriage, not only from the Royal Mail but also from other carriers. Certainly for heavy or bulky items, the chances are that specialised services will be cheaper.

> Tip: International couriers

Especially within the European Union, couriers can be by far the most reliable, cheapest and best option for sending your goods. As an example, I had to send a 6kg package to a friend in France. On a five-day service, that set me back £20. I think that's remarkably reasonable and affordable. It always pays to shop around when thinking about shipping, as International Air Mail from the Royal Mail is rarely going to be the best option for bigger or bulkier items.

Customs and exports

Sales within the European Union are blessedly easy: you might as well be sending items to Shoeburyness as to Strasbourg. For sales outside the EU, however, you need to fill in the appropriate green customs slip, so you'd be wise to get a bunch of these from the Post Office and complete them at home in your own time. This form declares the value of the item you're dispatching and whether the item is a gift or not.

Many buyers ask you to tick the gift box so they can avoid import duties. Needless to say, it is illegal to declare an item as a gift if it isn't.

Make sure you can actually export the items you sell to the country in question. There are all manner of arcane rules and restrictions that you may need to be aware of. For instance, the import of electrical items into Canada is restricted.

Language

If you have language skills that might attract international buyers, you should make a note of that in your item listing. A friendly word or greeting in a buyer's language may well be the clincher for an international sale. Language can sometimes be an issue, but many eBayers are happy to conduct a transaction in English even if it isn't their first language. If you don't have a common language between you, then free online translation services such as Babelfish or Google's Translation service can be helpful, but they aren't always accurate because they translate words literally.

Item Titles

If your items might have special appeal to residents in a particular country, it could be worthwhile including the relevant keywords in that language. This way when potential buyers search eBay you'll be in the results that are returned to them.

Payments

PayPal is the grease to the international trade wheel. It is simply the easiest international payment method and you can take payments from just about anywhere in a variety of currencies in the same way as you accept payment from UK buyers. If you do want to take other payment methods, make sure they carry the same protections and safety measures to ensure you don't find yourself out of pocket.

Managing expectations

Avoid confusion early on when trading across borders. It's best to overcommunicate and make sure there's no room for misunderstanding rather than assuming prior knowledge. Don't forget that as a seller you'll be the more experienced party in the transaction. Let international buyers know that postage costs and delivery time will doubtless be greater than within the UK and keep them informed if you know there are likely to be problems. People are very understanding if they're kept aware of what's going on.

SELLING SAFELY TO OVERSEAS BUYERS >

Two words sum up what's important here: PayPal and insurance. Only take payment by PayPal. That's all there is to be said: it means your funds are trackable and you're to some extent protected. In addition, when you're sending items overseas, ensure they are adequately insured.

One other thing you need by the bucketload is patience. There will be times when you feel like you're dealing with a buyer who's deliberately trying to make your life hell. Many international sellers I've spoken to say that sometimes it's just impossible to explain to some buyers why postage to Venezuela is much more than posting to the UK, for instance.

You also need to be firm. If you've made arrangements for payment to be possible by the means you prefer, and an international buyer wants you to take payment by a method you don't accept, feel free to insist on what you want. And needless to say, if someone claims to be the nephew of the former chief aide to the finance minister of Nigeria and wants you to ship a mobile phone or laptop to them on the promise of untold future wealth in gratitude, don't do it.

> Inside Information: The world is getting smaller

We've come a long way since Phileas Fogg made his wager at the Reform Club that a man could travel around the globe in 80 days. The internet has totally transformed how we live and work with our global neighbours. Nevertheless, sometimes it does seem that some of the old barriers and frameworks still exist.

Duties and customs remain antediluvian and a right pain in the ecommerce backside. Some countries have postal services that are quite simply not fit for purpose in the twenty-first century (and I'm not talking about the developing world: Italy's a culprit here).

But don't let this discourage you. International trade represents a source of profits and it's going to become more important. It's strange to note that currently only about 10% of eBay UK sales go overseas. eBay is keen to increase this and is actively encouraging more international trade.

Also, eBay is investing in new foreign markets. Most notably, it has opened a Russian operation that it hopes will be a successful new outpost in the eBay franchise.

The only real barrier to selling internationally is your own fear, so you need to get over it. Start small and limit your export nations. You're in control: if you want to limit your international sales to Australia only, you can. Just don't dismiss the idea of selling to people all over the world without experimenting – the potential rewards are simply too great.

14 | Why eBay sellers fail

Embarking on an eBay enterprise is by no means a sure-fire journey to success and riches. It seems fair to estimate that for every business that starts out and does well, two others will fall by the wayside and disappear.

I've asked two of the cleverest eBayers I know, Chris Dawson from Tamebay.com and David Brackin from stuffusell, to offer their viewpoints and ideas as to why eBay sellers fail.

BAD BUSINESS >

David identifies a lack of business acumen as one of the key reasons for some eBay businesses not succeeding. He thinks this is a particular problem for people who already know eBay and then try to turn that into a business. It seems that knowing eBay isn't the same as knowing business.

Such sellers, David says, 'exploit their good eBay knowledge with the zeal of a passionate individual and grow their pastimes into quite large businesses. But this is where the hobbyist can risk coming unstuck. I am often amazed at the number of people who have little clear idea of how their costs stack up outside of the direct material cost of their product.

'They know that their widget costs £10 and they sell it for £20,' adds David, 'but the details of exactly how much eBay takes and how to value their time and space elude them. Your own spare time and bedroom seem free, but once you get busy and start hiring people and renting space, the costs can quickly become quite real and painful.

'I've seen many become disillusioned with the hassle of the day-to-day of business management, which takes more and more time and is less and less fun, but which seems not to generate any more money than when it was a side project.'

BAD STOCK >

Not having the right stock in the first place, or failing to evolve as your best sellers become slow movers, is another reason eBay sellers fail, according to Chris.

'eBay itself changes. With the introduction of Top-rated Seller and changes to how eBay search works, the product which has been a bestseller on eBay might not be tomorrow. Products themselves change too. I know one seller of consumer electronics accessories who, as soon as a new iPhone comes out, sells off all his accessories for the last model at a cut price. He doesn't want to get left holding stock in a year's time for outdated models and, while iPhones are often handed down and there's still a market for accessories, there's more money and higher margins in accessories for the latest models.'

He adds, 'Make sure you're constantly searching eBay for your own products. Are your prices still competitive? Are your items appearing at the top of eBay search? Is the market for your products diminishing? Or is it time to source new product lines? I've seen whole categories on eBay move from being top-selling products to highly competitive and shrinking – and that doesn't only happen on eBay either. In the real world on the high street, think of music. The once mighty record stores have fallen and rather than buy CDs, many music lovers prefer to purchase MP3s nowadays. It's tough (though by no means impossible) to make money selling music online, and it's certainly tougher than it was ten years ago.'

Whichever category you sell in and whatever products you stock, you should always be on the lookout for changes and make sure you have the right stock to sell to meet those changes, whether that be a development in consumer buying habits, competition driving down prices or simply changes in the eBay marketplace itself. Change is inevitable, so you need to be prepared to deal with it.

As Chris says, 'Be ready for change and embrace it. The only constant I've seen on eBay in over 10 years of trading is that change happens and to be successful that means your business must change too.'

BAD eBAYING >

A great many eBay businesses never get off the ground because they fail to appreciate what a peculiar and nuanced marketplace eBay is. They simply transpose what they're doing already elsewhere and hope it will fly. The problem is that it seldom does.

David reckons this problem affects existing businesses who come to eBay having spotted the opportunity. 'Big businesses mistakenly believe they're building shops with shop fronts on eBay, but in reality each listing must stand alone and fight its corner in search. At this stage, these businesses feel that eBay is a disappointment and often abandon the marketplace: there is no volume because their listings aren't found. The next area where these businesses fail to adapt to the marketplace is dealing with the buyer. The eBay buyer is a needy beast, asking questions 24 hours a day and indignantly re-asking each hour that they do not receive a response. They are trained to blame the seller if anything goes wrong and wield huge power with their feedback and secret detailed seller ratings.'

I've seen this a lot too, not merely in new sellers, but in experienced ones too. It comes from having a set way of doing things and being unwilling to shift. I remember a discussion with a seller who'd been trading for some time and who sent his items out on only three days a week. As dispatch and delivery times became more important in feedback, his ratings fell. 'It's what I've always done,' he protested hotly and wouldn't accept that he had to change.

BAD BEHAVIOUR >

David and Chris were too gallant to mention this one, but it's vital to note. One reason eBay businesses fail is simply good old bad behaviour. A desperate seller might be bidding on their own items to get the price up (shill bidding) and get caught, for instance. eBay will banish that seller without hope of appeal in the blink of an eye.

Regular shoddy feedback or a string of unhappy buyers will also soon catch up with you on eBay: the powers-that-be will warn you first and put you on special measures. Then you have to be well behaved to stay on eBay successfully in the long run. If your copybook becomes too blotted, you'll be out on your ear.

Others fall foul of the tax man or are busted selling counterfeit goods or dodgy knocks-offs. Others fall out of favour with suppliers and stockists for being late with the bills. There are lots of ways to be badly behaved in business and eBay sellers can be as culpable as everyone else.

15 | The success roadmap

> There's a great deal more to ecommerce than eBay, but it's the best place to start and it's where you'll learn pretty much all you'll ever need to know about selling online. It's the home to multimillion-pound corporations, small family firms and businesses based from bedrooms. The book so far has looked at them all and how they succeed.

How you put into practice all the ideas and strategies I've discussed so far is very much your decision. Only you know what you want to achieve. Every plan will be different and every seller is different. Much of your success will depend on how much time and effort you put into your activities.

However, if you put reasonable concentration and industry into your eBay business, it is likely to follow a particular trajectory. The eight steps in this chapter digest my suggestions into a handy, stage-by-stage format and represent a success roadmap that's realistic for you to achieve over a three- to six-month period.

1> Find your feet

Your first mission, should you choose to accept it, is to immerse yourself in eBay and really get under the skin of what makes it work. You start by buying. Don't be shy about using search to find bits and bobs that you need and explore other categories. It's a good way to start poking your nose in and examining your potential competitors. You probably have a good idea what you want to sell, so find out how the others do that.

In particular, concentrate on what you *don't* like. Shoddy sellers do exist and you should take the opportunity to be better than them and to shine.

Part of finding your feet is also selling your first items. Clear out the cupboards, declutter the loft and get your junk on eBay ASAP. This way you can find out more about eBay, have a clear-out and also generate some funds that you can put towards setting up your business and buying stock.

2 > Sort out supply

Your first few weeks on eBay are going to be tough ones. At the same time as getting to grips with the site itself, you also need to take a firm hand on the tiller and work out what it is you're going to sell when you get the business up and running. This will take some groundwork and a bit of shoe leather as you do the rounds and find out what you can sell at a profit. Rest assured, it's the hardest bit of your eBay journey. So seek out suppliers, wholesalers, importers and the like and negotiate hard. You make your profit when you buy your stock at the right price. And use tools like Terapeak to help ensure you're not paying over the odds and are getting stock that has a solid profit margin.

3 > Hit the ground running

When you've got your stock, start selling it. It won't make you any money until it's up on eBay and available to buyers. Only then can the money start coming in. The first few weeks can be a bit painful for sellers because you won't have an established eBay selling record and your feedback and status won't be stellar. There's only one way to sort that: keep selling.

Take time to analyse your listings and make sure you apply a critical eye. There are always tweaks you can make to ensure that your descriptions, titles and pictures are even better. Keep a watch on the competition and make sure your prices are competitive, as well as paying attention to newcomers in your categories.

As each sale comes in, dispatch the item swiftly and make sure every customer is happy with what they're getting and so leaving you top-notch ratings. That's the only way to guarantee you get more visibility in search. Make sure you've always got some auctions running to maintain the interest.

4 > Prove the concept – or change it

If after a few months your idea simply isn't working, you need to divine why that is. Einstein defined madness as doing the same thing again and again and expecting different results. So if it's broke, fix it. Exercise your judgement. Is it that your business idea is fundamentally flawed, or is the problem that you've been too optimistic with your forecasts? It's very common for business plans to feature wildly overoptimistic sales predictions.

It could be that you aren't selling the right stuff or it could be that you're not doing some aspect of eBay in the right way. Don't let an early mishap discourage you too much. Think of it as a useful opportunity to finesse your plan and try something different.

If, happily, everything's going well and you're on course, keep on with what you're doing.

5 > Search for efficiency

Everything in your business can be done better in some way. Look at your working practices: can you save time? Look at your expenses: can you spend less? Examine your daily tasks: what is necessary and what can be stopped? Finding efficiency while staying effective is a balancing act, but you can always find improvements. Very often that means investment and getting better tools and software to help you along, but if your products are selling well, spending money to find more growth should usually be a no-brainer.

6 > Scale up

The greatest piece of advice you can employ on eBay is quite simple: list more to sell more. If you've optimised your operation, the best way to increase the size of your eBay business is to expand the scale of what you're selling.

That doesn't mean employing a goldrush mentality, however. What it does mean is applying the same analysis you did at the start when you established your business. Find more great stock lines to sell again, maybe seeking out additional suppliers and making sure you apply adequate rigour to crafting magnificent listings. And don't let expansion be a reason to become slapdash. You've got to grow and still keep the buyers happy.

It's in the growth phase like this that many eBay sellers lose their way. Don't be one of them. Keep an eye on quality and not just quantity. It's a real battle to double and even quadruple your output and maintain the highest standards of customer support, but it's one you can win.

7 > Measure, measure, measure

Is everything working as it should? Old, successful lines might not be selling as well as they used to. Is your courier still delivering the same service as before? What prices have gone up? Where is the next potential problem coming from? It's very easy to relax and think that all is well. But stay alert and keep watching the numbers. Don't be caught unawares because the price of widgets has gone through the floor or because there's a new competitor on the block selling them for half your price.

I've seen numerous eBay businesses fail because they weren't adequately monitoring their health. The problems made themselves evident in the end, but it was too late for anything to be done. The best you can do is make sure you have an early warning system ready for when the proverbial hits the fan.

8 > Go multichannel

If you've achieved all of the above, then it's time to start looking beyond eBay and planning to expand. Your first stop is likely to be Amazon. The good news is that the rest of this book is all about how to take your eBay business and experience out to other channels and marketplaces and continue to succeed.

Case Study | Why eBay sellers succeed | http://stores.ebay. co.uk/My-Invite-Designs

Shazina started selling on eBay in 2008. She'd left a full-time career in accounting to have and take care of her two young children and needed a flexible business opportunity so she could generate some much-needed cash quickly and work around the school runs.

She started the Personalised Party Company and has an eBay shop selling all manner of goodies and gear for holding a successful party. There's everything from children's party bag fillers to photo balloons, toys, fancy dress and of course personalised invitations and thank-you cards for every occasion. It's not just kid's stuff: she has supplies for birthdays, weddings, hen and stag dos, christenings and of course Christmas.

Shazina started the business from home and began by operating from the spare bedroom. First she invested in a specialist printer and materials so she could produce unique and individual items to order. Invitations and cards could have a friend's or child's photo on the front and all the messages could be original and bespoke to each order.

She was amazed that her business grew so quickly and soon she was running multiple printers all through the day just to keep up. By the end of 2009, she'd commandeered the garage and racked it out with shelving to contain her stock. Now, not only has she had to take on staff to keep up with demand, she's spread her wings to take on the Amazon marketplace and develop her own website.

She started selling on Amazon in 2012 and told me, 'Amazon is much better than I thought and it is proving to be as good as eBay for sales!' By joining Amazon she has nearly doubled the size of her business.

One thing that particularly impressed me about Shazina is her willingness to outsource important work that needs to be done to experts in that particular field, rather than bodging the job herself. She prefers to research the market and see who can do a task for her. For instance, her attractive eBay shop was put together with a unique design and personalised listing template by dZine-Hub. Her website is run by EkmPowershop and features a unique skin that integrates with multi-channel back-end software.

Shazina's business has gone from strength to strength in just a few years, to the extent that it has now outgrown her home. Taking premises was the only answer and that offered some choices in itself. In the end, she opted to open a retail premises rather than merely a warehouse or industrial unit. Now with a high street shop front, Shazina can take advantage of walk-in custom too.

Part II | Selling on Amazon, becoming a multichannel seller and lots more

It's time to broaden your horizons and look beyond eBay. This part of the book introduces you to selling on Amazon (a completely different beast), suggests and explains a variety of other marketplaces to sell on and also looks at the options you have when it comes to starting your own online webstore. It's all exciting stuff and it's all possible for a businessperson with enough verve and willingness to graft.

I also consider how to market and promote your webstore and products, as well as examining some interesting tools and services you can use to take your business into the stratosphere. Back on earth, there's a pile of vital information on tax, business registration and also the laws that govern ecommerce.

And then, I take a look at the future. What are the emerging trends in ecommerce? What will the world of online trading look like in 2020? Most important, how can you be ready to meet the challenges of one of the most infuriatingly ever-changing industries in the history of business? Last, and by no means least, I share some vital online resources that will ensure that when you're done reading, you won't be lacking in advice and ideas.

But that's a long way off yet. There's plenty more for you to find out and learn before the back cover, so let's press on.

16 | Multichannel selling challenges

> Moving from one channel to many can be a real challenge. Cracking eBay is one thing, but the expanding ecommerce enterprise must embrace multiple channels to really fly. You need to follow the buyers and make sure you have a ready supply of goods that are in demand.

There are four distinct challenges that you'll face as you diversify.

YOU NEED TO GROW AND STAY EFFICIENT >

Getting started is relatively easy and anyone can sell things and make pocket money. Indeed, it's an absolute doddle to sell and not make any money at all (and there are plenty of businesses which realise that after a year or so). But growing a business is a particular and tricky discipline.

It's rather like moving from juggling with three balls to four. As you make the transition, you aren't allowed to stop juggling and catching the first three balls. You must add the extra tasks to what you're already doing while keeping everything else in check.

So keep the wheels on. Do what you're doing already and do that better too. And then start doing something else entirely new that's at least (if not more) mind-boggling than what you're doing already. You bet it's tricky.

YOU NEED TO KEEP LEARNING >

There's always something new to learn: a new idea to apply or a different problem to solve. As I've said before, ecommerce keeps changing, and at an accelerating pace. That's difficult enough just on eBay, but as you face new and different marketplaces and web services, you're going to have even more to discover.

YOU NEED TO GET HELP >

It's eminently possible to run a business on eBay as an individual and keep it ticking over very well on your own with the various tools available. But going multichannel almost always means you have to open yourself up to getting some assistance.

For the most part that will mean finding a multichannel software partner who can help you manage your listings, stock, sales and dispatches across the board. There's a stack of advice on that later in this part of the book, but for now be aware that most people find this a challenging proposition.

By now you've got a seasoned ecommerce brain, so it's time to free yourself up from the most mundane of tasks and unleash your imagination to concoct future plans for your business. That's more fun and more valuable.

YOU NEED TO JUMP INTO THE BIG POND >

You know that eBay is competitive and you'll have learned some very valuable lessons there on how to be the best. But when you strike out, there's even more competition. On Amazon in particular, you sell alongside Amazon itself and that takes some wits. If you establish your own webstore, you'll be a tiny minnow in the whole sea of the internet, trying to get the attention you need to get sales. The sharks are every retailer on the planet with a website and Google's the killer whale.

The key is confidence. You must believe in what you're doing and know that what you're selling is in demand. You must also be clear about what you want. To make your efforts pay and turn the profits you need, you only need to gain a minuscule share of the global ecommerce spend.

If you're lean, efficient, dogged and imaginative, there's no reason why you shouldn't do very well. Ecommerce success isn't a myth. Businesspeople who have invested time and effort in their project have succeeded and you can too.

17 | Getting to grips with Amazon

An obvious key difference between eBay and Amazon is that the Amazon Marketplace is predominantly a venue for brand new goods. You can sell a few secondhand items such as books and music, but you'll struggle to build a business that way.

What sells best? The answer is just about anything you might be able to buy in a shop. Take a close look at the Amazon website, examining the category structure and browsing through the various departments. There are stacks of selling categories and Amazon is adding and developing these all the time, although it certainly isn't home to as broad a sweep of goods as eBay. Books, music and media are the obvious choices, but Amazon sells a very great deal more than that. Homewares, electronics, toys and clothing are also hugely popular with buyers. Almost 40% of sales on Amazon are made by third-party sellers.

Apart from selection, there are some keen differences to be aware of compared to selling on eBay.

YOU'RE SELLING ALONGSIDE AMAZON >

eBay itself doesn't sell any goods on the site, it just runs the marketplace. That's not true on Amazon. Amazon is a retailer in its own right: it sources stock, holds stock, runs warehouses and dispatches goods. So when you're selling on the site, you're competing with one of the biggest retailers in the world on its home turf.

Nevertheless, anecdotally it seems that Amazon approaches this situation with at least some decency, knowing that it can't squeeze out the small guys. Just before Christmas 2006, for instance, Amazon itself ran out of a particular brand of camera. Rather than not offering the camera to customers, it widely promoted a Marketplace seller who still had stock to fill the gap.

THERE'S LESS OPPORTUNITY TO PERSONALISE >

One of the reasons Amazon is so easy to use is that you incorporate its preprepared descriptions into your listings. For example, when you sell a DVD you simply put the EAN (barcode) number into the site and Amazon fills in all the details for you. This is handy, but it makes it very hard for you to stand out from the crowd and differentiate yourself from other sellers of the same items.

IT'S A PRICE-SENSITIVE MARKET >

It's the difficulty differentiating yourself from other sellers that makes price so important on Amazon: being cheaper is one of the few ways you can stand out. The way in which Amazon displays products favours cheaper items. The site also determines the postage costs, so you can't be more competitive in this aspect either.

Julia Priddle of ChannelAdvisor describes the experience rather well and draws the distinctions with selling on eBay:

'Amazon owns the experience. Amazon takes great pride in managing the entire shopping experience for its buyers. The company is understandably very protective of this customer experience and, if it feels that marketplace sellers are not delivering the level of service that Amazon expects, they can penalise or terminate that account. If you are going to sell on Amazon, you therefore need to respect these simple rules. Shoppers must stay on site. A fundamental part of the Amazon experience is that customers should not be directed away from the site.

'For marketplace sellers,' she says, 'this means that any sales transactions, advertising or other means of communication with Amazon shoppers that would direct them off Amazon are strictly prohibited. Even having a link to your webstore on a product listing or description field can be viewed as grounds for being dropped from Amazon.'

And that echoes one thing that I have heard again and again from Amazon sellers. While eBay can be tough, Amazon is super-stringent.

REGISTERING ON AMAZON >

Getting started on Amazon as a merchant can be time-consuming and tricky. Amazon screens and vets every seller and you'll be required not only to verify your details but to prove that you're the kind of seller the company wants on the site. This can take weeks or even months. There will be forms to fill out and many people don't get approved the first time they apply.

In the end, if you want to sell on Amazon this is something you'll have to live with. On the other hand, it means there's less competition from other sellers. You can find out more about registering with Amazon here:

> http://services.amazon.co.uk/services/sell-online/how-it-works.html

There are two other things to be aware of on Amazon as you go to register. The first is rather annoying. Amazon operates a more 'closed garden' selling environment to that of eBay. With one eBay ID, you can buy and sell around the globe. That's not so on Amazon, unless you sign up for a premium service.

When you register as a seller in the UK, you can sell only on Amazon.co.uk and you'll need a UK address. To get your goods in front of the massive buying audiences in Germany, France and the rest, you'll need to register with the relevant Amazon site. It gets more complex than that too. To trade in those countries you need a postal address there, business credentials and often a local bank account. None of these hurdles is insurmountable, but it does mean more paperwork and hassle.

Secondly, when you register on Amazon, you need to choose which package suits you best. There are two: Basic and Pro. The difference between them lies in what you can sell, how much it costs to do so and the tools and facilities available to you.

If you think you'll be selling fewer than about 30 items a month, then plump for Basic. You'll pay 75p per listing and then also pay what Amazon calls 'per-item selling fees'.

If you're a serious ecommerce seller with a solid track record behind you on eBay, then the Pro package is probably going to be more appropriate. There's a subscription of £25 a month (you can cancel at any time and you get the first month free) and you don't pay a listing fee, but you do have to cough up selling commissions.

There some other perks to the Pro deal. More selling categories are available, you can access the bulk listing and tracking

tools Amazon offers and you have the chance to be a featured seller. As a Pro customer you can also take advantage of the Amazon 'Jumpstart' programme, which is described this way: 'Even with Amazon's user-friendly tools, uploading a large catalogue to sell on Amazon can be challenging and take up valuable time. Learning the system, understanding the requirements, and uploading your inventory are time-consuming unless you have specialist help. With Amazon's new Jumpstart service, we can help you get up and selling in no time. Our team of trained listing professionals will prepare your Amazon listings following Amazon's own best practice guidelines. Please note that a minimum of 100 listings is needed in order to benefit from this service. These listings can then be uploaded onto Amazon.co.uk and, if listings for identical products already exist, even Amazon's 4 additional European Marketplaces (Amazon.de, Amazon.fr, Amazon.it, Amazon.es).'

It does sound as though this could be well worth the subscription fee alone, which varies depending on how many products you list. Full details are available here:

> http://services.amazon.co.uk/jumpstart/pricing.html

GETTING READY FOR A SUCCESSFUL AMAZON SALE >

You can choose which category your item will appear in (there's a choice of about 20-25) and you need to find the Amazon-provided description using a barcode number or keywords. Once you've found the catalogue information, you specify your price.

Items don't expire on Amazon, so your products can remain available for as long as you like. When your stuff does sell, payment is taken by Amazon via its in-house system called, unsurprisingly, Amazon Payments. The company deposits your takings directly into your bank account on a 14-day cycle, after taking its cut.

Amazon is very clear on your responsibilities as a seller and prescribes the postage costs (which are typically passed on to the buyer) and how you should mark and address the envelope, as well as giving clear guidance and instructions on dealing with particular issues. You can view that very exact guidance at:

> www.amazon.co.uk/gp/help/customer/display.
   html?nodeId=3149411

There is a feedback system on Amazon, but it's different from eBay's in several ways. First, while there's no facility for you to rate buyers, they can rate you on your performance using a scale of 1-5. Feedback is also not as important and integral to the trading system as it is on eBay.

FEES >

You'll see a theme emerging when it comes to fees for the various marketplaces: they're complicated. Amazon makes it a bit easier than some of the others, as its variations largely occur in the size of the commission selling fees. These fees differ greatly, from 9.2% of the sale price for gaming consoles through to an eye-watering 40% for Kindle accessories (it's safe to assume that Amazon wants to keep that sector to itself and is discouraging other sellers with massive fees). Some (but not all) of the selling fees are lower if you sign up for a Pro account. The full rack of fees can be found on this page:

> http://www.amazon.co.uk/gp/help/customer/display.html?nodeId=3149301

INSIGHTS INTO AMAZON >

Selling on Amazon is dramatically different from selling on eBay. Here are a few comments that sellers who have migrated some of their sales to 'the river' have made to me.

Winning the Buy Box

If you've used Amazon as a buyer, you'll know that it directs buyers to sellers much more than eBay does. The Buy Box is that bit of an Amazon page where you've settled on the item but not quite decided who to buy it from: the Buy Box shepherds you to the sellers Amazon likes best.

You really do want to get to the top of the list (or as near as possible), but everyone else want to win the Buy Box too, so it's competitive.

Ecommerce blogger Matthew Ogborne explains the function of the Amazon Buy Box: 'Unlike eBay where you can have multitudes of the same item over many listings, Amazon's format is different. Amazon has one "master" listing and then allows multiple sellers, including itself, to sell that item.

'This master item contains information that is an amalgamation of data from eligible sellers of the given item, although some master items are created by Amazon itself and contain more in-depth descriptions than it allows merchants to create.'

So as you trade on Amazon, keep an eye out to see which of your products get into the Buy Box. As is so often the way, we don't exactly know what determines who achieves this, but there are some obvious factors you can focus on.

The price of the product is important (although Amazon doesn't always promote the cheapest), but you're also assessed on how you've performed in the past and how satisfied your customers have been. So buyer reviews and how many complaints have been made about you in the past become significant: poor performance can really dent your profile in the Buy Box. Amazon also likes to see that you have sold the item in question before and kept consumers happy. Using Amazon FBA (of which more in a few pages) is also a good way to assist in your quest for the Buy Box, because Amazon will be controlling the dispatch process.

Bagging the Amazon Buy Box is something you'll have to graft away at for a while until you hit the jackpot, because you have to prove to Amazon that you're a good seller. However, once it is satisfied, you'll find that the Buy Box can have a dramatic and positive effect on your sales, so it's worth fighting for.

You can find out more about the Buy Box on Amazon here:
> http://www.amazon.co.uk/gp/help/customer/display. html?ie=UTF8&nodeId=200408180

Less sophisticated tools

While Amazon is geared up for merchant sellers, the day-to-day management a seller has to do on Amazon is much less than on eBay. The company takes much more of the strain. This is of course reflected in the fees it takes and also in the lack of control a seller enjoys, but it's also seen in the tools available to sellers. Many people say that Amazon's selling tools are less sophisticated than the ones eBay makes available. Of course, this won't be an issue if you swiftly adopt a multichannel selling partner who will help you manage your inventory, listings, dispatches and the rest. Such services are examined in detail later in Chapter 19, 'Multichannel software'.

Selling booze

It's nothing to get that excited about, but Amazon has different rules to eBay, which means that some things that are banned on eBay are allowed on Amazon. Have a look at the sales categories for more information. Just as an aside, for no other reason than that it has excellent sections for wine and whisky, I'll mention that one big difference is that Amazon allows you to trade in drink if you're properly licensed. Hic.

Completely different relationship

People still talk of the relationship between seller and eBay as a community-based, warm partnership (although many sellers don't feel this is the case in reality). With Amazon, it's quite simply a business relationship. eBay sellers who've migrated say that they like the stark honesty of the relationship without the schmaltz. Many buyers will be unaware that they're buying from a third-party seller when they commit to buy, so it can have huge merits. At the same time, it's no wonder that Amazon is so interventionist.

Steady sales

Amazon sellers report that they can pretty much bank on their sales through that channel. The site obviously markets hard and promotes certain lines, but if you're not selling the hottest, in-vogue items, then after a while you'll probably be able to predict from week to week what you're likely to sell.

Strong seasonal surge

The surge of custom in the run-up to Christmas is reported to be huge and more dramatic than on eBay. This should hardly be a surprise. Amazon controls the process more keenly (and also spends masses on marketing at Christmas), so it can guarantee last-minute delivery with more aplomb. People will believe it and order in their droves.

> ### Tip
> In Chapter 7, 'Managing your eBay sales', I suggested you use Terapeak to keep track of marketplace trends on eBay. You can also use it on Amazon and it's highly recommended.

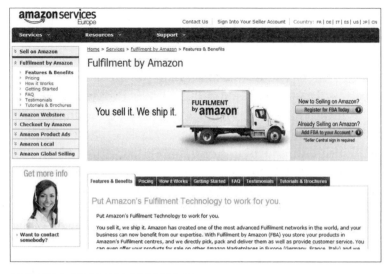

FULFILMENT BY AMAZON >

Obviously, Amazon has warehousing, staff and processes to store and dispatch its own items quickly and officially, and it has an excellent reputation as a fast shipper. It should therefore not come as a surprise that it offers these services to merchants at a price through a service called Fulfilment by Amazon. It works like this: you send your goods to an Amazon warehouse and it stores them for you. If and when they are sold, Amazon takes care of dispatch with its usual alacrity. In fact, Amazon will fulfil any of your orders for any marketplace.

It's a great service. While naturally it attracts some fees, they could well be worth paying when you consider the costs of doing it yourself. Impressively, Amazon claims that FBA customers see a 30–40% uplift in sales because the programme comes with some perks:

> Eligibility for free Super Saver Delivery and Amazon Prime for FBA Listings on Amazon.co.uk.
> Use of the prominent 'Fulfilled by Amazon' message, making your FBA listings more attractive to buyers.
> Ability to sell on the French, German and Italian Amazon Marketplaces from a single inventory pool in the UK.

Consider the costs very carefully, though. There's a warehousing fee for every month your goods are in the Amazon warehouse and also an FBA fee on top of the Pro selling fees you'd normally pay. In total, fees stack up to somewhere in the region of 30% of the sale price. There is a download that explains the FBA fees at:

> http://g-ecx.images-amazon.com/images/G/02/images/ FBA_UK_RateCard_EN_Nov2012.pdf

For more about FBA in general, go to:

> www.amazon.co.uk/gp/help/customer/display. html?ie=UTF8&nodeId=200292880

SAVING TIME AND MONEY BY BEING EFFICIENT >

One of the very clear distinctions between selling on Amazon and on eBay is the time you spend managing your listings. On eBay, a great sink of time will be devoted to making sure your product descriptions and photos are up on the site and available. You may have listings ending at certain times, a mix of auctions and BINs as well as aspects of your shop that need tending to and organising.

The good news is that you don't have this kerfuffle on Amazon. You simply tell the site via the sell form what you have to sell (and it has to match what's in the catalogue), how many you've got and what price you want for them. The items then stay up for sale until they're all sold.

This means that the search for efficiency and effectiveness on Amazon must be more keenly focused on the back-end operations of your business. If you're maintaining your eBay sales alongside those on Amazon, one of the real timesavers is going to be a multichannel management tool to streamline your operations. I talk more about such programs in Chapter 19, 'Multichannel software'.

Obviously, as with eBay sales, consider your carriage costs and services carefully, but primarily as a multichannel seller you need to stay organised. Technology can help here, but good old-fashioned discipline in work practices – as outlined in Chapter 10, 'Saving time and money by being efficient' – can make all the difference.

> Inside Information: Surf the Amazon

Since 2006, Amazon has been growing fast, largely fuelled by its successful integration of third-party sellers. The site didn't begin as a person-to-person marketplace like eBay, but it has taken a leaf out of eBay's book and successfully brought business sellers within the fold. Now you're just as likely to be buying from an independent merchant as from Amazon itself.

This is good news for consumers, who benefit from the competition and a greater selection of goods for sale. It's also good news for ecommerce professionals, as it makes Amazon a totally different outlet for sellers, attracting buyers who might not use eBay. If you can, sell on Amazon as soon as you feel you've cracked eBay and while you're hungry for growth.

Amazon and eBay will doubtless both continue to survive and compete. To be able to enjoy success in both is a remarkable opportunity. And if truth be told, your operations for both are likely to be almost identical. When it comes to succeeding you'll need the same skills, efficiency, stock and gumption.

Different goods sell better or worse on each marketplace, so part of your task is ensuring you've got the right products selling in the right place. Helen Parker, CEO of the bulk wholesale and clearance marketplace Stockshifters, gives an example: 'One of our biggest traders reported, "We had 200 laptops that had been on eBay for weeks. We posted them on Amazon, at a higher price, and they were all sold within days at a higher return, even after fees." But a clothing buyer who recently purchased a clothing lot from a top retailer stated, "I made the effort to try Amazon, but it didn't really work. I then tried eBay. I've now sold half the stock in 4 weeks, and am already in profit."'

Case study | Profit from FBA | http://stores.ebay.co.uk/BTR-Direct | http://www.btrdirect.co.uk/

Bryn Morgan has been selling DVDs online for more than seven years. It's his full-time job and he also employs some people part-time if he needs them. On eBay he's a Top-rated Seller with more than 30,000 unique feedbacks and he's an Amazon seller with his own website too, powered by Amazon Webstores. He's also been experimenting recently with other lines such as toys.

Bryn says the secret to selling successfully online is to find products that have very strong margins and where possible to be one of very few sellers in a particular niche. Discovery Channel titles have been the backbone of his business. He's cultivated a strong relationship with his suppliers and often has exclusive rights to certain titles.

He continues to sell on eBay and Play.com, but has found they aren't as strong for him as Amazon.

He's also devoted to Fulfilment by Amazon for his Amazon and webstore orders. He says that with FBA 'you become Amazon', because to the customer it looks just like an Amazon sale. In addition, as Amazon promotes FBA items (because it can guarantee the service provided), it's much easier to get to the top of the search results and have the all-important 'buy box'.

Bryn strongly advises other sellers not to dismiss FBA simply on grounds of cost. He notes that it has real benefits when boosting Amazon sales and also means you can cut other costs such as staff and warehousing. It also saves him a stack of time, so is a particularly useful service if you experience a surge in sales.

Bryn also has a word of caution for anyone wanting to start their own website. He invested in one a few years ago and declares it a mixed experience. He found it was a better use of his time to invest in new lines, source better stock to sell and fully maximise the potential of Amazon than to spend it promoting his website. He says, 'People head straight to Amazon or eBay and trying to get enough attention for your own webstore is very difficult if you're a small business.'

> Let there be no doubt: eBay and Amazon are the joint titans of ecommerce for anyone who wants to build a resilient and robust business that delivers profits. If you can find a win on them both and keep going (a key test is surviving the bustle and struggle of two Christmases), then you're doing something right.

Nevertheless, there are other marketplaces available and they are worth exploring. You'll need to exercise your little grey cells once again and make a discerning choice regarding where your efforts are best placed.

ETSY >

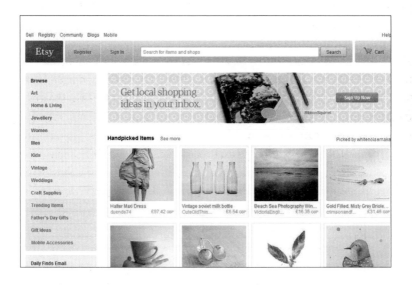

For my money, the most exciting and adorable smaller marketplace on the block is the ever so kooky and original Etsy (etsy. com). Founded in the US in 2005, it remains a relatively homely, almost villagey, place to shop. But that is to underestimate the site's size and scope.

It has over 25 million members, 850,000 sellers, 18 million items for sale and 60 million visitors stopping by to shop every month. In 2012, Etsy enabled trade worth $895.1 million all over the world. It's a big deal – but what's the attraction?

Etsy is packed full with what could be called craft items, although that's not all. Anything that's original, artistic, retro, vintage, handmade or created is to be found there. We're talking fashion, art, jewellery, ceramics, textiles and almost anything else you can imagine. Take five minutes to check the site out and you'll see what I mean. I promise you'll be addicted if you like pretty, decorative and handmade things.

Like so many other people, I find this an inspiring and enjoyable place to search for gifts for friends and original items. Many of the sellers are stateside (which isn't an issue, as most will ship to the UK), but a burgeoning number are in the UK. My shopping list over the past year or so has included cards, prints, a really lovely Kindle cover and a scarf. Another boon is that PayPal is the main payment method.

What Etsy does so well is to present the goods that are for sale. Pictures really matter and the best are really shown off to their full effect in search and on the homepage. The feast of visual imagery serves to draw the buyer and browser in to sate their appetite on the beautiful and eclectic things that proliferate on the site. This is something eBay sadly lacks – searching for items there has become a chore and is a tawdry business. Etsy has managed to make it a joy and it remains serendipitous. More often than not, you'll end up buying something you never knew you wanted.

And Etsy's super-friendly too. Descriptions are chatty and positive. The feedback system is not so very different from eBay's, but the whole tone of the website and the experience somehow manages to remain light and exciting. Etsy is a bit hippy-like, so if you go there you might want to wear a flower in your hair.

The low-down for sellers

Etsy is a specialist marketplace. If you're a scale seller on eBay and Amazon, sourcing stock to sell and not making your own stuff, it's not going to be much help to you. That said, if you're creative and are constantly busy making something fabulous, it has massive potential.

Etsy is clearly a viable outlet for some business areas. For instance, it's a favourite destination for cute and quaint wedding items, and original or personalised clothing, artwork and the like do well.

The upshot is that you can easily turn your ecommerce skills to Etsy and use it to make some money if you're selling something that suits the site, but it's unlikely to start generating a big chunk of your bread and butter any time soon.

NOTONTHEHIGHSTREET.COM >

One of the fastest-growing websites during Christmas 2012 in terms of the numbers of buyers it was attracting was relative newcomer to the ecommerce scene Notonthehighstreet.com. The name gives you a fairly solid clue to what the site seeks to do. It sells gifts, nice things and unique lines that quite simply aren't to be found on the high street.

From a seller's perspective, you need to have goods that Notonthehighstreet.com wants to showcase on the site and that aren't freely available elsewhere (so that's a new challenge). In addition, the site requires you to provide your business bona fides.

So far it boasts an inventory of over 50,000 beautiful things and is continuing to grow. It's a great site, with a good buying experience and some really wonderful items, so check it out.

For more information go to:

> https://www.notonthehighstreet.com/join/signup

RAKUTEN/PLAY.COM >

Rakuten is a huge Japanese internet company that you probably haven't heard of, but you will be seeing more from it soon. It has great potential to be a big player in the ecommerce field and it's currently on some sort of buying spree and snapping up various firms in the field, so keep your eyes open for developments.

One of its first acquisitions is a site you may well be familiar with, play.com. This specialises in selling tech items, entertainment-related goods and also computer kit. If you're trading in those areas, it's well worth checking out. As it stands, it's unlikely that Play will make up a decent chunk of your turnover, but sales are sales and many of the multichannel software packages will plug your inventory in with ease, so it could help you boost the bottom line. Play also provides some interesting shop features that can help you trade independently and also market to users on Google.

Overall, what is clear is that Rakuten is a company that has big plans, even if it's currently unclear what that evolution will be, so keep watching what it does.

FLUBIT >

This new marketplace has only been around for a year or so but is already boasting multimillion-pound sales and is set to have a bright future if all goes well. Flubit (I have no idea how you pronounce it) is a slightly different buying and selling experience from eBay and Amazon.

Here's how it works. Buyers cruise the internet looking for things they want to buy. They find the product somewhere and then take the link (copy the URL) and give it to Flubit. From its network of merchants, Flubit scans to see whether an identical item is available and then tries to find the hopeful buyer a better price. In a sense it's the ultimate comparison shopping engine, but from a buyer's perspective it gives them a lot more power to choose what they want to buy. Find out more at:

> http://flubit.com/

STUBHUB >

StubHub offers a marketplace purposefully honed to the sale of tickets for gigs, events, concerts and sport. The company was bought by eBay some years ago, which means that eBay is withdrawing from the ticket market altogether on its main

marketplace. This is understandable. In a highly specialist field, eBay was open to massive scrutiny and often bad press when tickets were sold for more than their face value. That said, buying and selling tickets is big business and plenty of sellers make a good living from it.

StubHub boasts a policy of 'making it good' for customers if a problem does occur. This means for sellers that they no longer have to worry about the equivalents of Top Seller ratings, feedback or DSRs. StubHub guarantees all transactions between buyer and seller.

It also takes away a lot of the grunt work. StubHub handles all the customer contacts and provides you with a shipping label so you can send the tickets on. For sellers there are no more customer emails or dealing with other logistical issues. Inevitably, this attracts a charge.

Sellers pay a single fee for sales and that includes PayPal costs. There's no listing fee at all, only a selling fee, which currently sits at £25 for casual sellers. If you want to sell a load of tickets, the word on the street is that you should contact the StubHub seller support team by email at sellerservices@stubhub.co.uk.

Check out the site at www.stubhub.co.uk. Information for sellers is available here:

> https://sell.stubhub.co.uk/sell/

> Tip

This section highlights the biggest and most significant of the alternative dedicated marketplaces for sellers aside from eBay and Amazon, but it's by no means an exhaustive list.

Keep your ear to the ground for other players. Clothing sellers should remember that ASOS has a marketplace, for instance.

CLASSIFIEDS >

For a business, it might seem counter-intuitive to suggest that you have a go and see what you can get out of online classifieds, but it's nevertheless a good idea. Traditional classifieds that used to be found in newspapers are typically favoured by consumers selling one-off items. The classified format has been transferred online very successfully, but not by newspapers. It's been famously pioneered by the kooky web phenomenon that is craigslist (www.craigslist.com).

Craig Newmark started this site in San Francisco and it has spread around the world very successfully. Despite overtures from many of the big players, and despite being valued at billions of dollars, craigslist remains independent. The service is largely free to advertisers (there are some fees in jobs and property sections) and is likely to remain so.

This is a model that has been successfully taken on by a whole host of imitators. The best-known version in Britain is probably Gumtree (www.gumtree.com), which is owned by eBay, but there are dozens of others. Promoting your sales and your website is about getting the traffic wherever you can find it and channelling it to where it can make you money. Classified sites are buzzing with visitors and traffic, so see what you can get out of them. Certainly consider advertising individual items or lines and make sure that you get links back to your own website.

COMPARISON SHOPPING >

Comparison shopping sites are web destinations that aggregate information from other internet-based shops and online sellers and present it to buyers in an intuitive and easily approachable way. So if you want an electric toothbrush and you go to a comparison shopping site, you'll be presented with information from a variety of vendors about similar products. The idea is that you can then easily view and compare different sellers and as a consumer make the best choice.

It's a popular and successful model that is appealing to buyers because it's the online equivalent of 'shopping around', but without the hassle of schlepping down the high street and popping in and out of every relevant shop before returning to the first one you went to because it really did have the best deal. Consumer champions such as Martin Lewis of www.moneysavingexpert.com often promote the use of comparison shopping sites as the best way to bag the biggest bargains.

Comparison shopping sites don't actually sell anything: the transaction itself takes place on the vendor's website. Comparison sites make their money by charging sellers for the traffic they send to sellers' sites. It's done on a cost-per-click model, so sellers only pay for the people who click through to their website. In some ways, comparison shopping sites are a throwback to an age when search engines weren't so good and it was easier to go to a specific site to do your shopping, but even so, they are still popular and effective.

Because of their popularity, the big comparison shopping sites provide an opportunity for sellers that is potentially more lucrative than other eBay-like marketplaces. However, because of the way the process operates for sellers, they aren't suitable for everyone. They work best for competitive areas of commerce where price matters more than anything else.

Getting your inventory onto comparison shopping sites is pretty straightforward. You provide up-to-date information about your products, and when your items are clicked and a customer comes to your site from the comparison shopping site, you pay a fee.

Nevertheless, the cost-per-click model has its challenges. For instance, it means that you pay even if the person who visits your site doesn't buy anything.

Comparison shopping sites are also pretty cagey about what they charge. This is because there isn't a level playing field where everyone is charged the same. They operate on a more traditional, commercial model, meaning that if you're a big player with deep pockets, you can doubtless negotiate a very good deal. As a small-time seller, you might not find that the door opens quite so easily.

If you decide that you're interested in tapping into comparison shopping traffic, you're probably best to contact a site directly to get information on terms. One benefit of this more conventional approach is that when you're up and running you'll probably be allocated an account manager who you'll be liaising with as you develop your sales.

Kelkoo

Kelkoo (www.kelkoo.co.uk) claims to attract 10 million unique visitors every month, making it one of the most visited shopping sites on the web after eBay and Amazon. It's also the biggest comparison shopping site in Britain. According to the company, Kelkoo only charges you when a user clicks through to your site after choosing one of the listings you offer.

Each category has a different minimum cost. Your offers and shop will appear more prominently depending on popularity, relevance and the fee you pay.

In terms of getting your products onto Kelkoo, you have two options. You can choose a free Product Feed Upload, where

Kelkoo helps sellers produce a file in a special format that can be uploaded every night. Or for a fee you use the Kelkoo Spider to scan your site and list your products automatically.

You can find more information about how to list your items on Kelkoo at:

> http://www.kelkoo.co.uk/co_4292-online-merchants-and-stores-partner-with-kelkoo.html

Shopping.com

Shopping.com is another big player in the comparison shopping market. eBay bought the company in 2005 because it wanted to broaden its portfolio of ecommerce sites. It was also attracted to the huge number of member reviews and the wealth of product information the site held.

When you sign up with Shopping.com, you send the site a list of products to promote. You manage your expenditure on a category basis, rather than having to deal with large numbers of keywords. There are automated reports and a free ROI Tracker to help you track the cost of your sales and maximise your profits.

Find out more at:

> http://uk.shopping.com/sc/advertising-opportunities

19 | Multichannel software

> The aim of this chapter is to help you find the multichannel software partner that's best for you and your business. It's one of the bigger decisions you'll ever have to make as an ecommerce entrepreneur, but the rewards you can obtain are genuine. If you can harness the right software to give your business a massive boost, you'll see a step-change in how you trade online.

BENEFITING FROM A SOFTWARE PARTNER >

You could manage your multichannel business using the tools and interfaces that each individual marketplace provides. You could log in each morning to My eBay to see what had sold on there and then head over to Amazon and check what success was waiting there. You could generate all the invoices and packing slips and off you'd go to pick and pack. But that would be ludicrous and waste you so much time and effort that in the longer term you wouldn't be able to cope.

It's essential to cross the Rubicon and embrace a multichannel partner who can help you streamline your ecommerce business and ensure that you can grow further in the future.

> Tip
> There are a multitude of management tools on the market and there's not enough space to look at them all here. You can find a more comprehensive list on Tamebay:
> http://tamebayguide.com/management

CONSIDERING A MULTICHANNEL MANAGEMENT PACKAGE >

The problem is that at first glance all the providers look rather similar and it's difficult to ascertain what each does differently.

Having worked with or met many of the people in this industry over the years, it becomes obvious that in reality the firms that do the multichannel thing are very diverse and individual. The characters of the businesses themselves, the people who work there and what they strive to do are all variable. And in fact, the main aspect you need to think about really is whether you can do business with these people.

So, once again, take your time to assess the various services and be very sure that the one you choose is truly going to be able to help you transform your ecommerce enterprise. It's pretty much the biggest strategic decision you're likely to make at this stage and it would be best to get it right. Don't go with the flow or make an instant call. Research, research and research again.

The only absolute piece of advice I can offer would be to go with a company that's based in the UK or at least has UK operations. The British scene in ecommerce is suitably distinct from that in the US that on-the-ground UK experience is vital. This leads to another key suggestion. You're about to make a huge investment of time, effort and money in dealing with the company in question, so it makes sense to meet the people who run it if you can.

Ten companies are showcased in this chapter for a reason: one size doesn't fit all. You have to make the final decision based on what you want and need. Here are some factors to think about as you approach the problem.

What do you want your business to be?
If you've got a good business going on eBay and are just at the stage of considering Amazon, then you're likely to want expertise and help to embark on that for starters. But if you're already an

advanced seller on Amazon, what you really need is someone who can help you move on elsewhere.

So when you're thinking about the various options available, be clear in your mind about what you need right now, in the short term, to make the change pay. Some services are honed to already established businesses that need streamlining. Others offer an on-ramp that will help you scale up. Part of the choice you face is knowing what you want and need.

Don't assess the firms by what they offer and what they claim to do. Think about them in terms of what they can do for you to help you achieve your goals. That means you need to be clear on what you want to do in the first instance.

Which markets do they support?

This is a fairly obvious point, but one that shouldn't be neglected. You'll probably want eBay and Amazon for starters and as standard, but what next? Not all multichannel firms support every marketplace. So if you fancy some action on Rakuten or Flubit, do check that the company offers that facility. Some firms will say 'it's in the pipeline', but pipes can be very long, so it would be wise to find out how long development may take.

Then check that the offering is optimised for the particular sectors of the marketplace you predominantly use. High-volume, low-value sellers require different support to those who do high-value, low-volume sales. Get to know the multichannel product being offered as best you can before you invest time and money in it.

Do they help sellers like you?

The marketing blurb that many multichannel suppliers provide is dominated by information about the big names they support. That can be a useful reckoner and also shows some prestige, so there's no reason to dismiss it. But you aren't a blue-chip big-name FTSE company; not yet.

It's best to ascertain whether the company has someone on the books who looks like you and does something similar to you.

And if possible, try to have a conversation with that person too. Nothing beats a real testimonial from someone who does something like you and is already using the product. Furthermore, it pays to be suspicious if the firm can't find you someone to talk to.

What do they cost?

This is obvious, but it's also worth thinking about for a while before going 'ouch'. Charges for this kind of software vary widely and can be based on a monthly subscription, a percentage of total turnover or indeed an à la carte menu for particular services. At first glance, none will seem cheap despite the fact that charges vary widely.

Needless to say, you get what you pay for. So if you want super-spiffy support, that is likely to cost more than a download where you're left to yourself to muddle through. But think of the price in terms of what the service might help you achieve. If you get a 20% uplift or more in existing sales and manage to generate more profits and additional sales, the fees may seem much more attractive than they did initially.

Judging the costs is another occasion where it really pays to know your business metrics inside out. Only if you understand what's going on will you be able to judge what you can afford.

Have they got the functionality you need?

Just like with a car, you want some sort of test drive in the form of a demo from the multichannel company. It's the only way you can judge whether the service has the facilities you need and is something that you (and your team if you have one) can live with and use with ease every single day. Most of the services will be quite complex and intricate, so it's alright to be bewildered at first. But do make sure that the kit does everything you require.

Again, work out in advance what it is you need in order to take your business to the next level. The checklist will vary from business to business, but make sure that the firm you take on covers the essentials, if not some of the nice-to-haves. And consider other functions of your business that could prove to be useful.

Design, accountancy, stock control and other facilities could offer the scope to streamline your operation and could well be available too as part of the package.

Equally, don't be wowed and seduced by things you don't need. The company may have an impressive menu of seemingly vital services, but if you don't need them they shouldn't form part of your decision.

How good is their customer service?

This aspect is critical and should be informed by your experience with eBay. It's inevitable that things will go wrong from time to time, so be sure that when they do, you can get someone on the phone sharpish. In the first instance, get a clear idea from the sales rep of what sort of support is offered. Then get the skinny from an existing customer for a reality check. Scour the web for forum comments and reviews too, although it's wise to take a balanced view. Online comments tend to focus on the negative.

Can you get out?

It's always worth planning your escape, so make an agreement with the provider that can be broken at your convenience. There are two reasons this might become vital. It might be that your relationship with the company doesn't work out and you don't get the business growth you might have hoped for. That does happen. Just make sure you can move on with the minimum of hassle and bad feeling.

The other reason you might want to find another supplier is that you outgrow the service and need something with a bit more poke. That's good news and you'll want to transition your business to the next supplier with as little fuss as possible.

> Inside information: Not just software, but business partners too

Your choice of multichannel software partner is a critical one for the future of your business, so take some time to fully appreciate the different options on offer. If you boil this down to the bare bones, you're looking for a company you can enjoy an easy and positive relationship with that blossoms over the years.

The best in the business are collaborative and take a collegiate approach that suggests they're as interested in growing your business as you are. They will be living ecommerce day to day in the same way that you are, so they ought to be fizzing with ideas and strategies that can be used to help you. When you start considering this sort of business consultancy and advice as part of the package and price, some of the prices start to look positively reasonable.

10 MULTICHANNEL SOFTWARE PROVIDERS >

Check out this list and see which firm leaps out at you to investigate further.

Brightpearl | www.brightpearl.com

This relatively new service has been making waves in the ecommerce industry since it opened a UK operation in 2012. Brightpearl boasts that its 'robust cloud-based platform enables retailers and wholesalers to efficiently connect customer demand with product supply across all their channels of sale: in-store, online, 3rd party marketplaces such as Amazon and eBay, over the phone, and even temporary sites like kiosks and pop-up stores'. Subscriptions clock in from £69 a month, but extras like telephone customer support cost an additional £20 a month.

ChannelGrabber | www.ChannelGrabber.com

The guys at ChannelGrabber position themselves as a great-value multichannel software solution. Based in the UK, they support eBay, Amazon, Play.com (Rakuten) and your own webstore, and the software can help you list, manage your orders and track your inventory across different channels. In terms of cost, the basic package (say if you're listing 5000 items at a time, maybe 100 orders a day) will set you back £60 a month. More advanced offerings are also available.

ChannelAdvisor | www.channeladvisor.co.uk

For many years now, ChannelAdvisor has been helping eBay sellers develop their business and it was one of the first firms to develop multichannel software to take sellers from eBay to Amazon. Led by professorial CEO Scot Wingo, CA always seems to have a finger on the pulse of ecommerce and is a true expert in the field. It certainly has one of the most comprehensive offerings and is able to assist with search engine optimisation, web marketing and the like as well as ecommerce. ChannelAdvisor also stages the annual Catalyst event in London, a key part of the ecommerce calendar. Fees will depend on what level of service you take, involving a monthly subscription and a percentage commission on fees.

eSellerPro | www.eSellerPro.com

This born-and-bred UK firm 'integrates a retailer's entire online sales process, simplifying and automating tasks such as inventory management, product listing and scheduling, sales order processing, payment and dispatch, customer communications and accounts posting, saving time and money and leaving businesses free to concentrate on service and customers'. eSellerPro boasts some fairly impressive existing customers, which indicates it's a solution that's going to be best suited to bigger sellers and retailers. It already serves BMW, Tefal, Argos, Maplin and Office. The service is optimised for eBay, Amazon, Flubit, Rakuten and Google. Depending on the service you take, eSellerPro charges a start-up fee and then a monthly management fee.

Lengow | www.lengow.co.uk

If you fancy looking at some new areas, such as selling on Facebook and other social networks, Lengow might have the offering for you. US in origin but with British operations, Lengow offers a rather more rounded suite of marketing tools to ecommerce traders and also helps you track and optimise your campaigns. These guys also integrate with osCommerce, Joomla and the comparison shopping engines. Subscriptions start from £99 if you have somewhere in the region of 500 distinct items or lines in your catalogue.

Linnworks | www.linnworks.com

More than 2000 ecommerce sellers are using Linnworks already and that's not surprising. The owners, based in Chichester but with Estonian roots, are young, bright, ambitious and clever technologists. They offer a basic multichannel management service for a monthly subscription, you can end the contract whenever you want and if you have ambitions for something really big, they can develop you a bespoke package. Well worth checking out if you want to work with some ecommerce geeks.

Neteven | www.neteven.co.uk

French business Neteven provides something slightly different and is worth considering if the focus of your business is already European or you want to develop your enterprise that way. Thinking about Europe as a trading bloc can reap rewards, although it's an option that few people embark on. The other distinct feature of Neteven is that it offers you an à la carte menu of options (that must be because it's French), meaning you simply choose what you want from the myriad of sites, feeds and marketplaces the company supports across Europe.

Seller Dynamics | www.sellerdynamics.com

This UK company serves eBay, Amazon, Rakuten (Play.com), FNAC (big in France, Belgium and Spain) and will also slot into a Magento store if you develop one (see Chapter 20, 'Building your own webstore'). As it says of its service: 'Seller Dynamics is an easy-to-use, time-saving system enabling you to monitor the performance of your entire sales operation from a single web-based dashboard, and manage dispatches to customers in a powerful and timely way – all the while saving time by automating a whole range of everyday tasks.' Also on offer are 'automated competitor monitoring and dynamic price management to instantly respond to any marketplace changes, ensuring that your offerings are always competitive'. Such flexibility will prove to be vital in fast-paced marketplaces.

SellerExpress | www.sellerexpress.com

SellerExpress has several features that will attract the canny ecommerce entrepreneur with an eye on growth. First, it has been assiduous in optimising its products for the different international markets on eBay and Amazon, so it's a good bet for sellers who want to make an overseas splash. Second, it offers a 30-day free trial. In this arena, that's a good offer to make sure you can get the software to work for you. SellerExpress is optimised for Amazon UK, USA, Germany, France, Spain, Canada, Japan, Italy and Spain and integrates with eBay UK, USA, Germany, Ireland, Spain, France, Italy and Australia. It also serves Rakuten (Play.com) and webstores powered by EKM Powershop, Volusion, Big Commerce and Magento. The company is based in Northern Ireland and the basic bundle starts at £50 a month.

Storefeeder | www.storefeeder.com

The clever aspect of this company is that it provides all sorts of seamless integration with a number of companies, all with the aim of making your trading life easer. And it doesn't just hook up with loads of trading websites (there's an impressive list on its website), it also offers integration with UK couriers such as Royal Mail and DHL (to name a few) so that the dispatch end of your business is hyper-effective too. Storefeeder packages start at £100 a month and are worth checking out.

> ### Inside Information: Fulfilment
How would outsourcing great swathes of your business appeal to you? For services similar to Fulfilment by Amazon, companies exist that, for a fee, can handle most of the logistics of a multichannel ecommerce operation: everything from holding your stock to processing your orders and dispatching the

goods. In fact, all you need to do is sort out your supply and deal with customers.

This kind of option requires a mammoth leap of trust and can cost quite a bit. However, when you consider the time you might spend on doing these activities yourself and the expense of staff and warehouse, you might find it makes sense. The fulfilment company will essentially be in charge of your business reputation, but equally, some of them offer a really bravura service. To enable you to check out some of the offerings, there's a list on Tamebay:

> www.tamebayguide.com/fulfilment

Case study | The benefits of multichannel software | www.spy-cameracctv.com

A business trip to Hong Kong set Lee Adams off on ecommerce. He stumbled across a neat little camera while browsing a market stall and snapped up a dozen or so to sell when he got home. A few months passed before he sold them on eBay, but he was pleasantly surprised by the profit he made, so he set out to find a supplier and now he runs his own business retailing CCTV equipment and cameras. He sells on eBay, Amazon and also through his own website, and for the past few years has seen both his business and his profits grow.

Nevertheless, setting up his multichannel business was far from plain sailing. 'With a bit of trial and error,' says Lee, 'I kicked off my ecommerce business by setting up my website SpyCameraCCTV. My business was getting bigger and bigger and after a while it became clear that I needed something more robust supporting my business than my current software if I was going to scale this growth effectively.

'We were using a concoction of Sage Line 50, Excel Spreadsheets and Google Docs. We had become inefficient. Sage was too slow for us with multiple users, understanding spreadsheets became increasingly more difficult and Google Docs were in overwhelming abundance.

We couldn't expand and grow with Sage, which essentially is just an accounting package. Along with a multitude of systems going at once, we had no customer management system and a complete lack of automation. This led to miss-picks, double selling, lack of communication and wasting valuable time. We were inputting data twice and my motto is if you have to do the same thing twice you're doing it one time too many!'

In the end, Lee opted for Brightpearl and has found that taking on a multichannel solution has revolutionised his business. 'Having orders, inventory, accounts and customer data in a single system is unbelievably helpful and reduces the time it takes for us to make decisions or automate processes considerably. We are able to concentrate on growing the business rather than implementing and managing multiple disparate systems.'

All in all, with the elimination of mistakes, a leaner operation and indeed staff costs, all told Lee reckons that the system saves him £45,000 per annum.

> For many small businesses trading online, building and honing an ecommerce website that is dedicated to your organisation constitute a giant leap. This may be when you truly feel ownership of what you do and make some serious money, but I should sound a note of caution. Your website is going to take a while to find a life of its own. So before you start, prepare yourself to be patient and make sure you can keep your eBay and Amazon sales ticking over too.

Building the site itself will take some time (depending on how you choose to create it), and it will then require more time to start indexing and performing well in search engines. Your marketing is unlikely to kick in overnight and even when the site is attracting buyers, generating sales, making you money and everything is tickety-boo, it will still need maintenance, love and attention. A website is always a work in progress.

Don't let that put you off, though. Lots of sellers are already doing it successfully and they don't necessarily have any experience of running a website. In fact, if it's of any consolation, I meet very few sellers who regret setting up a webstore. Most of them regret not having done it sooner.

You have three options when it comes to building your website. The path you choose depends on your technical know-how and the sort of website you want. If you have the skills, you can build your own site. This option offers you the opportunity to create exactly what you want. If you don't have the skills but want a site that's personalised and bespoke to your needs, consider hiring someone to do it: there are countless individuals and companies that offer this service and you shouldn't find it hard to locate someone suitable. The third possibility is buying an off-the-shelf shop that you can customise.

The technology has come a long way in the past few years and the customisable services now available offer some sophisticated options for ecommerce sellers. They come in all shapes and sizes and can cost anything from a few hundred pounds to many thousands. The choices you make will depend as much on your budget as on your preferences and ambition.

CONCEPTUALISING YOUR WEBSITE >

Whichever path for developing your own webstore you decide to take, you need to be very clear about what you want. You can be imaginative and individual here, but remember the aim is to sell as much stuff as possible, not to act as an outlet for your quirkiness.

1 > What do you like?

Take some time to surf around the web and identify the kind of sites you like. Think specifically about those you enjoy buying from and make a note of why. It could be the navigation (how you're guided around the site), the way pages are laid out, or how you're led through checkout to complete the purchase. What you like counts for a lot. First, when it comes to your own site, you're more likely to be proud and confident of something you think looks good and that means it's more probable you'll make a success of it.

Second, if you like something then the chances are that other people will like it too. In the absence of the huge research budgets companies such as eBay possess, you have to trust your instincts and experiences when it comes to building a winning website.

2 > What do you need?

At some point in the process of building your own site, you have to construct a brief or requirements document. This will explain to you, or whoever builds the site, exactly what the site is intended to do and look like. A very good start, early on, is to determine exactly what the site needs. You obviously want a homepage of some sort, but what will it do? Display items? Talk about your company? How will shoppers know what you've got for sale? Should you have a search function? Do you need a checkout function? How will people contact you? Will there be different pages for different products? Make your list and decide which aspects are 'must haves' and which are 'nice to haves'.

3 > Look and feel

Whole libraries full of books have been written about the theory and practice of web design and what works and what doesn't. If you ask five web designers what a good website looks like, you'll get at least ten contrasting answers. Go for a website look and feel that you like and that are reflective of your business and what you sell. Again, look at other sites to confirm your preferences. There are a few factors worth bearing in mind, though:

> **Avoid too much clutter**   While stark, white minimalism isn't required, do avoid the opposite. Chintzy, cluttered sites with busy backgrounds and no obvious structure are difficult to use. When there's too much going on, people won't be able to get down to shopping. You should also be mindful of the visually impaired, who find lurid websites difficult to navigate.

> **Use images**   Pictures are a must. Whether they're of products, you, your premises or anything else relevant, they bring your business and website to life. It's not difficult to produce a really engaging, image-rich site and with the growing use of broadband, you don't need to worry so much about slow download times when people visit your pages.

> **Have clear calls to action**   Make sure that people know what to do and where to go to buy and pay. To make certain things stand out, ensure they're big enough. To make them stand out even more, make them red as well.

CHOOSING A WEB ADDRESS >

Giving your webstore a good URL or web address is essential. Your first instincts will probably be to name it after you or your business or to give it a quirky, maybe funny, cute or punning name. That's what we're used to: it's how shops have been named for years. High streets are full of shops called 'Wilson & Sons' or 'Wilson's Laundrette' or have pen shops called 'His Nibs' or fish-and-chip shops called 'The Codfather'.

But when you set up shop online and you want to attract as many searchers as possible, being practical and straight-forward works best. For instance, Bobthebrickie.com isn't as good as brightonbuilders.com. It's similar to when you chose your eBay User ID. Match your URL to what people are searching for in your particular area of business by using these tools:

> https://adwords.google.com/select/KeywordToolExternal
> http://inventory.overture.com/d/searchinventory/suggestion

They tell you what the most popular keywords are and also make suggestions for other words you might consider.

WEBSTORE SOLUTIONS >

When it comes to building the site itself, numerous compa-nies offer webstore services. The basic rule of thumb is this: the greater the cost, the greater your opportunity to customise. This is a fast-moving area of ecommerce, so don't be afraid to seek out your own supplier or solution. The best way to do this is to find an online store that excites you and see who has developed it. There's usually a link at the bottom of the page.

The big players in the field are:

> Magento   www.magentocommerce.com
> X Commerce   www.x.com
> Amazon Webstore http://webstore.amazon.co.uk

All these companies operate in a similar way and are well worth exploring if you're already a sizeable trader and want a highly sophisticated and robust webshop. What the big three all offer are the ecommerce guts of a webstore.

You sign a licence and have the right to use the company's back-end technology to power your outlet, but that's only the start. On top of this ecommerce machinery, you need to put your design and preferences. Here's where you'll either need to do it yourself or, more likely, engage a specialist developer and designer to do it for you (I talk more about how to do this below). You'll determine the look and feel, the categories and how things look to your buyers, as well as all your product details. And behind the scenes, the software does its job.

These services are sophisticated. Xcommerce is owned by eBay and obviously Amazon is behind the Amazon webstore. The licences themselves are not expensive (and the cost is determined by usage), but getting a developer to sort it all out can be a significant spend. One seller I spoke to recently didn't think it was possible to get a really good store with much change from £5000. And remember, there will be ongoing maintenance to pay for too.

OFF-THE-PEG SOLUTIONS >

By far the cheapest and easiest way to get a webstore up and running is to choose one off the peg. These solutions obviously have limitations and won't suit the needs of a big merchant, but they're a good starting point for a typical ecommerce entrepreneur. They're also a good way of proving the concept of your website. You can easily spend thousands of pounds on a webstore and it would be a terrible waste if it turned out that you couldn't make it work.

So if you start with one of the following options you can limit your outlay and be certain you have the ability to make the best of a webstore. After that, with a great deal more confidence and a heap more experience, you can make the leap and build the glitzy store you've always dreamed of.

Firepages | www.firepages.co.uk

This UK-based firm offers off-the-peg ecommerce webstores for a fixed price. The one-off fee starts from £399 and the company also provides other support services such as web marketing and hosting.

VisualSoft | www.visualsoft.co.uk

At a slightly higher level, Visualsoft provides ecommerce webstores plus design and other services from its HQ in the northeast of England. Costs vary depending on your specifications.

Ekmpowershop | www.ekmpowershop.com

One of the most popular providers of webstores, Ekmpowership offers many cool features. Packages start from £19.99 a month.

Create | www.create.net

This Brighton-based company already hosts and provides over 10,000 online shops. The most basic option starts at £2.99 a month, with additional features upping the cost. This is definitely a good option for a smaller trader.

DOING IT YOURSELF >

If you have the skills and expertise to build a website, then that's the obvious choice. It's fair to say that when you create a site as complicated as an ecommerce shop, you won't be building the whole thing from scratch. You'll probably be building a 'mash-up' and combining different bits of functionality. For instance, you could embed a search functionality from Google, a checkout from PayPal or Amazon and videos from YouTube or Revver to create an enticing offering for your customers.

You might also be interested in a selection of resources that come recommended from sellers who've already set up shop: osCommerce (www.oscommerce.com) offers a menu of open source features that you can use for free and is well worth exploring.

HIRING SOMEONE >

If you're lucky, you already know of a person or a business who is capable of building your site. If you're even luckier, you might have a bright spark working for you who can do it. But if you need to search for a developer, what you're really after is a recommendation.

You may be able to find someone local in the phone book, or you could check out Elance (www.elance.com), an online space where professionals and businesses like you link up to do jobs for each other. The systems the site has in place mean you have a clear agreement with the service provider regarding the job that needs to be done, as well as safety mechanisms to protect your payment. If you go through Elance you need to construct a good brief for your service provider to work from. One benefit of the site is that it provides reviews and comments from previous clients on the work the provider has done. Like on eBay, this gives an invaluable insight into whether you want to do business with this particular person.

But whoever you select, make sure you plump for someone who can communicate with you. In my experience, techies aren't very good at talking to the rest of us. Many of them think that we should speak their language and they tend to be poor at communicating in any other way. It's often all PHP, Ajax, My SQL and gig this and meg that. If you're having difficulty understanding what they're saying or doing for you, ask them to explain. You're the customer and you should know what you're paying for.

Just getting a website built and up and running isn't enough. You need to promote it in various ways too, and that's what the next chapter considers.

21 | Promoting your webstore

Once your website is up and running and open for business, it's time to get people through the door. It's a fair bet that your site has fixed costs, so the more sales it makes, the better the profits. If your site is built and ready but simply sitting there not making sales, it's losing you money.

Chapter 22, 'Search engine marketing', considers the ins and outs of marketing on the mighty Google, but I start with some other promotional options that you might also want to try.

MARKETING ON eBAY AND AMAZON >

Marketing your own website on eBay is tricky. Needless to say, eBay doesn't want buyers and sellers going elsewhere. You can't, for instance, have your website address as your User ID or eBay shop name. And when it comes to linking to your own shop, the links policies that eBay provides do little to explain what's allowed or disallowed. In fact, it's all absurdly confusing. See for yourself at:

> http://pages.ebay.co.uk/help/policies/ia/rules_for_sellers.html

There's one thing you definitely can do and that's put a link to your shop on your About Me page. You'll get some traffic that way and it's good for search engines too. But do not on any account put links to your own website in your listing pages: that's the fastest way to get kicked off eBay. This kind of tactic isn't allowed on Amazon at all.

The easiest way to market to an engaged, positive and eager customer is to grab their attention when they've just bought something from you. That's why your eBay and Amazon customers are a key target for your marketing. At the very least, include a leaflet or flyer with every dispatch to let your buyers know you're also selling from your own site. Make the leaflet as good as you can. A print-out will do, but a well-designed, printed colour flyer is better. Just check out eBay for sellers of A5 colour printing: you may be surprised how reasonable it is to get 500 or 1000 leaflets. And you may find an even cheaper deal online – another job for Google.

Make sure your URL or web address is prominent on the leaflet. Also, ensure your sellers are in no doubt that you're open for business and ready for them to come shopping. You can tempt them to visit by telling them about any special sales or discounts you have available on your site. It's really worth having a popular line that you're selling more cheaply on your own website than on eBay (but not Amazon, where you need to be aware of price parity) as a draw, so you can say 'Things are cheaper on my website!' with pride.

Additionally, in every email you're sending out via eBay or Amazon, make sure you have a link and a call to action: Visit My Website! Consider putting the URL of your site on the exterior of your packaging and anything else you can think of that a customer receives. Be shameless. Check out what Packvertise offers if you want to be a real tart:

> www.packvertise.co.uk

EMAIL MARKETING >

A mailing list is an important marketing tool to help you move forward with an ecommerce business. Once you have your own site it's a vital means of staying in touch with your customers. In fact, if by the time your site is up and running you haven't already got a mailing list going, you need to get started on one quickly. Building a mailing list takes time, but it's absolutely time well spent.

You might already have experimented with mailing lists and used the facility made available with your eBay shop. If, however, that list is starting to number more than a few hundred email addresses, it's time to begin administering the list yourself. It's a valuable asset and you need to keep it in your own hands.

The legal regulations for building and maintaining a mailing list are pretty straightforward. You can invite people to join your list and they have to opt in to that list. I repeat: subscribers have to actively join your list. It's not acceptable simply to add an email address you've acquired (maybe that of an eBay buyer) to your list, send them an email and then take them off the list if they ask you to. They have to opt in.

And in every email you send out, you must provide subscribers with the option to be removed from the list and you must do that if people ask. You can find out more about the law relating to email marketing here:

> https://www.gov.uk/marketing-advertising-law/
  direct-marketing

In terms of getting people to subscribe, you can simply ask them to email you requesting to be added to your list, or have a special page on your website where they can submit their email address. Make sure you prominently promote your mailing list on your site and in your general admin emails too. It's also worth thinking about adding a box in your checkout process that people can tick if they want to receive your mailings.

Making the most of your mailing list

Building the mailing list itself is only part of the challenge when it comes to email marketing. You also need to think about what you're actually going to send out. The best way of maximising the value of your mailing list is to send your subscribers emails they want to receive. That sounds easy, but it's surprising how many emails I receive that don't have me in mind.

A good email reminds people that you're still there and doing business. Some successful mail-outs don't even have a sales-driven tone or a specific pitch: they merely include news. Others highlight offers, bargains or new lines.

Below are a few more pointers about email marketing.

The content should be right for your business

You've already spent time building a brand and a website that succinctly represent you and your business. Make sure that these carry through to your marketing emails. What you're writing should be correct and accurate. Emails with text only are fine, but using graphics and images is better and is more likely to be compelling to readers.

The content should be right for your customer

Targeting the message of your email to the recipient is critical to generating a favourable response. Someone who bought a pram last week probably doesn't need another one this week, but they might well want something else related to a baby. You know your customers better than anyone else, so go with your gut instinct.

One seller I know sent a Christmas ecard to his mailing list thanking his past customers for their business over the year and saying he was hoping to serve them again in the New Year. It was a well-designed email with a friendly tone, and was completely uncommercial: no offers, no prices and no call to action. It generated more custom than any other email he has sent before or since.

Playing by the rules

If someone wants to unsubscribe from your list, they want to unsubscribe. No arguments. Make sure you take them off the list promptly and don't email them again – ever.

Not overusing the list

Have you ever joined a mailing list and subsequently been bombarded by frequent, even daily, pointless email messages? Annoying, isn't it? Don't send too many emails, because it not only alienates subscribers, it also dilutes the potency of your message. It's surely better to generate a big wave of orders from one email rather than five trickles from five separate emails.

Timing is everything

Getting the timing of your emails right involves two aspects. If an email is promoting time-sensitive lines (say for Christmas or Valentine's Day), make sure you give subscribers enough of an opportunity to size up your offers and respond. Don't be too late and miss the boat. That said, too early is just as bad, because people won't think what you're promoting is relevant.

It's also worth thinking about what day of the week you send your emails out and what time of day they arrive. You may want to avoid Monday mornings when people often have overflowing inboxes, but what's most suitable will depend on your customers and you know them best.

FACEBOOK AND TWITTER >

Social media has made a big splash in recent years. Facebook has one billion users around the world and Twitter is a regular feature on the evening news and a source of stories and comment for journalists. Businesses cannot ignore the possibilities these two social media giants offer, but equally they represent a challenge and require a specific set of skills and expertise to utilise them properly.

Whole books could be (and have been) written about how you can use Facebook and Twitter to your advantage. This short section is only going to look at a few ideas. In the first instance, remember what these sites represent. They're a useful opportunity for you, but they don't in themselves form a marketing strategy or panacea for your business. They are options on the menu and they won't be attractive to everyone.

There is also a temptation to sink too much time into social media, because such sites can become slightly addictive. That's why it's a good idea to have in mind a strategic goal when you use Facebook and Twitter, because just sitting at your machine (or fiddling with your mobile) keeping a constant watch on your feeds is a total waste of time. Liking posts and tweeting trivia aren't going to pay the bills either.

Facebook fan pages

It's relatively easy to establish a Facebook fan page and it's a good opportunity to include links to all your various trading outlets – eBay, Amazon, website – wherever they may be. You can then invite all your friends to like the page and use it as a place to advertise what you're up to and any special events and promos you might be holding. It's tricky to get cut-through though. Facebook is noisy and getting anyone's attention is hard, so it's unlikely that you'll attract hundreds and thousands of followers like the big brands do. Also, if you don't have that many friends personally, it can be difficult to attract any more than a handful of followers.

Advertise your Facebook page in your product dispatches and emails to customers and your total will edge up over time. The more fans you have, the more things you can do with the page to benefit your business. One thing Facebook is very good for is communicating with your most loyal and enthusiastic customers and keeping them informed and close to your business.

Facebook advertising

Facebook also offers advertising, which can be a a boon if you've got a small budget and something specific to promote. You can choose to pimp your ad to Facebook users according to their profiles and interests.

So if you want to market to men in their twenties who like Doctor Who and Jesse J, you can easily target your ad to them. You can also hone the ad specifically to particular geographical areas. I recently set up an advert for an event that was aimed squarely at people who like 'theatre' in 'Brighton' and it enjoyed a very favourable and cost-effective response. You set a budget and you're totally in control. It's well worth experimenting by spending a few pounds advertising some specific products.

The jury is out as to how much trade Facebook really drives, but it seems inevitable that the site will seek to maximise that source of income in the years to come as it looks to generate greater profits. Understanding how Facebook works is therefore likely to prove to be good training for the future. Facebook is here to stay.

Twitter

Twitter is a completely different beast to Facebook and is a social network that rewards effort and input over time. The major problem is that when you start on the site, it can seem as if you are shouting into the abyss and no one is listening. That's because you're doing exactly that. The major challenge is to garner some followers and be part of conversations that matter.

It takes mere moments to set up a Twitter account and to brand it beautifully. Then you've got to start saying things. Begin by sharing articles or blog posts that you've enjoyed and are perhaps relevant to your business. It's vital to start talking from the get-go. Next, start following other people. Connect with people you know, those in your local area, others with similar interests and for fun, see if you can find any favourite celebrities who tweet.

And then just keep going. Tweet me if you like (@wilsondan) – if you say you've read my book, I'll be sure to follow you back. Twitter becomes much more interesting when you have several hundred followers or more. Catch people's eye by commenting on what they tweet, offering an opinion and also sharing what others have written with your own followers. That's called 'retweeting'.

When you have a following, you can start sharing business messages and information on what you're selling. Don't do it too frequently or brashly, because that can annoy people. But it's not a breach in protocol: plenty of people promote their businesses actively on Twitter.

Much of the hard work on Twitter can be done in spare or quiet moments and it need not eat into your working day. Download an app to your smartphone and on your commute, or when you're waiting for something, use the dead minutes to have a look on there and post something. Little and often works well on Twitter. Make regular contributions and your follower tally will tick up.

Measuring social media auccess

As with a lot of marketing, it's hard to know what's working and what's not with social media. Use an analytics program to track whether your activities are generating any traffic or sales and amend your activity accordingly – try simplymeasured.com for some free reports. However, the best way to approach social media is to do it because you enjoy it. That way, and this is especially true on Twitter, it's not a chore and hopefully your enjoyment will shine through and attract more followers.

LOCAL MARKETING AND PR >

Don't neglect the good old-fashioned ways of marketing when it comes to promoting your website. Never leave the house without a small stock of your own flyers, leaflets or business cards emblazoned with your web address, to give out or leave where people will find them. You might also want to consider getting posters made and asking relevant places to display them. Little things like this can be an integral part of building the momentum of your site.

Paying for print advertising is usually expensive and it's difficult to assess its success. So if you want to get in the papers, try to do it for free. Commenting on relevant stories by writing a letter to the editor for publication (including your URL) is worth a try and you may also want to attempt to get featured in articles. You've got a good story to tell – you're a businessperson, branching out, doing something different – and other people will want to hear about your enterprise. Look for opportunities to contact journalists who've written articles that you could have featured in and tell them your story for future reference.

Try to get on the radio as well. Phone-ins are a good means of doing this, and if they're relevant to you as an online seller or eBayer, so much the better. It shouldn't be hard to get a plug in and promote your site. You build up your site traffic and sales on your website through lots of little bits of marketing. When you were an eBay seller, eBay did all this. Now you're on your own you have to do it yourself, so take on the challenge with good grace.

PROMOTING YOUR WEBSTORE CHECKLIST >

> **Market your site to your eBay and Amazon buyers** Make the most of your existing customers and alert them to your site.
> **Build a mailing list** Start gathering email addresses and building a mailing list as soon as possible – it takes time to achieve something meaningful.
> **Unleash your emails** Reach out to those on your mailing list in a structured, respectful way to drive sales.
> **Don't neglect traditional marketing** Make the most of your story and the people you know to promote your website.

> ### Inside information: Affiliate schemes

Once your website is up and running and you're getting clicks, traffic and customers, you might want to think about signing up to some affiliate schemes. These are a way of making money out of your traffic by sending people to other websites. Traffic – the people who visit your site – is the most valuable commodity on the internet. Lots of big companies are willing to pay good money if you send some of your traffic their way. It's not necessarily going to make you a pile of cash and it's not really easy money, but it could be a good way of adding a few quid to the bottom line.

You may think you'd be mad to promote other websites, and you might have a point. After all, you've worked hard to build up your traffic and sending it away might seem like madness. But doing it right won't mean losing your hard-won traffic. Rather, it's about sending people who aren't going to buy from you elsewhere and making some money out of them anyway. You can promote things you don't stock or even push products that bear no relation to what you do sell. You'll probably be amazed by the variety of businesses you can promote in this way.

Different affiliate schemes work in different ways, but all are based around the same principles. You include on your website a banner, link or other ad for the other site. When someone follows the link to that site and does what they're supposed to do, you get some recompense. Some schemes are only looking for traffic, others want to acquire customers and only cough up when you send someone who actually joins the site, while others will reward you if your customers buy something.

You'll be rewarded in different ways. Sometimes you get a few pence a click, or maybe a little more for a longer visit. The bounty for helping a business acquire a new customer will usually be more, maybe a few pounds (or more for potentially very valuable customers). If you're paid based on sales made by the people you send, that could be a percentage of sales or a revenue-sharing model.

Some companies administer their own affiliate schemes, such as Amazon:

> https://affiliate-program.amazon.co.uk/

eBay's scheme can be found here:

> https://publisher.ebaypartnernetwork.com

Many also outsource their programmes to third parties. The two biggest and most respected agencies in the field are Commission Junction (www.cj.com) and TradeDoubler (www.tradedoubler.com). You can sign up to these services and they will keep you up to date with the latest offers and promotions.

One of the reasons having your own website is so potentially lucrative and vital for a professional seller is the astonishing number of people who start their online shopping with a search engine. When a potential customer searches on Google, they may not necessarily have a destination in mind. That means they're ripe for the picking – they could become your customer.

There are two ways of making the most of this opportunity and ensuring you have a profile in search engines. The first is to have a site that is the most relevant in relation to what people are searching for, so that it appears at the top of the search results. This is called 'natural' or 'organic' search. The second option is to get your wallet out and use the 'paid for' options, enhancing your visibility with sponsored links.

WHAT'S THE GOAL? >

The ideal outcome for your business is good placement of your website on the search engines. You definitely want to be in the first page of search results, and ideally you want to be one of the first three on the page, up at the top before the point when searchers need to scroll. Depending on the keywords you want to be found with, this is eminently possible.

Of course, large companies all know this too and destinations like Amazon, eBay and the comparison shopping sites spend astonishing amounts of time and effort optimising their websites and outlaying vast amounts on search engine advertising. You may not have the same budgets or person power as the big boys, but here's the good news: you can do the same.

Optimising your site for search engines is relatively straightforward, as I shall explain in a moment, especially if you build the requirements into your original brief and construct a website that search engines will like. Making a start on paid-for search engine advertising is also pleasingly easy, but requires management over time and you need to develop some expertise here. You can't afford to let the obstacles put you off: harnessing the power of search engines is critical to your success – it's an absolute 'must do'.

Let me state the bleeding obvious: Google dominates the internet search market. As a result, I've centred this section around the services that Google offers. Be aware, though, that there are other significant search engines, such as Yahoo! or Bing from Microsoft. None is as big as Google, but all of them are worth investigating and all of them have similar services that you can plug into.

SEARCH ENGINE OPTIMISATION >

The idea of search engine optimisation (SEO) is uncomplicated: making your website as accessible and attractive as possible to search engines. This in turn enhances your natural search performance and you show up well in search results without paying for that profile. The idea itself may be self-explanatory and most of the techniques laid out here are simple too, but it's astonishing how many sites haven't been adequately optimised.

Once you know the tricks, it's easy enough to spot the mistakes other people are making. An unoptimised website is a terrible waste because it means that the people who want to find you can't do so.

> Tip: Don't pay extra
When you're deciding on a website package or service provider, don't pay extra for SEO. It's often peddled like snake oil and that should be enough to get your antennae bristling. If someone asks you to add SEO on to a standard package, the chances are that they're not the best person for your job. It's like buying a car and the car dealer asking you to pay extra for the steering wheel. Request search engine optimisation as standard – full stop.

Making sure your site can be read

The first step in search engine optimisation is making sure that the spiders that search engines send out to catalogue and index all the sites on the internet can easily read your site. Ensure that your site is free of 'frames' that block the spiders. Sometimes a developer will use blocks of images that fit together and look lovely to readers, a tactic often employed for glossy, glitzy headings on websites. It looks good to people, but not so good to the search engines, so try to strike a balance in your site design.

Helping the spiders

The way your site is crafted is also important in the sense that there are ways of telling the spiders what they want to know in a form that's beneficial to you. If the spiders understand what your site is about, they can categorise it properly. If you're not familiar with HTML or coding, this may all seem a bit bewildering, but do try to get your head around it. Even if you're not going to code your site yourself, the concept is worth knowing about and it'll mean you can communicate your needs to your developer.

How Google works is a secret. Much of what people talk about as being best practice in the field of search engine optimisation is speculation and educated guesswork based on testing and trial and error. Nevertheless, a great deal of argument still occurs about what's important and what's just froth and nonsense. The best advice is to cover all the bases and consider everything that might have a bearing on your success. Here are some areas to consider:

> **URL**   We've looked at the importance of your URL already in terms of communicating with buyers, but the web address of your site is important to the spiders too, so make sure it reflects your keywords as well as possible.
> **Title**   The title of your page is what you see at the top of the browser window. It's just a short description of the site and page you're on. This an opportunity to describe your page again with your keywords. In HTML the coding is something like this:
<TITLE>Put your keyword rich title here</TITLE>

> **Meta tags**   You have another opportunity to describe your business in the site's meta tags. These are not visible to people viewing your site, but can be read by spiders (although opinion is divided about what importance the search engines imbue them with). The HTML for your meta tags will look something like this:
> <META NAME="DESCRIPTION" CONTENT="Put descriptive sentences here describing the page. Don't forget the keywords!"> <META NAME="KEYWORDS" CONTENT="put,your, Keywords,here,separated,by,commas,not,spaces">

> **Headers**   Just like in a book, you organise your site text with headers that signal to readers what certain sections are about. How you code those headings helps the spiders understand what the sections are about too. Using the H1, H2 header tags in your HTML tells the spiders that the text they are reading is a header and therefore more important than the other words, so they can pay more attention to it.

> **Alt text**   This is text describing what an image is about. It's good practice to use it, because people with visibility problems who use page readers to surf the net go to the alt text to 'read' an image. Spiders also use the alt text to understand what an image is because they can't see pictures, therefore they do attach importance to it. Make sure you fill in the alt text field for any pictures you're using and don't leave it empty.

Building keyword-rich content

Search engines love the written word. It tells them what your site's about and when they should offer it to searchers. So provide plenty of what internet folk call 'content'. However, reams of pointless rambling aren't going to do you much good. What you need is keyword-rich content that's relevant to what you're selling.

Like on eBay, keywords are the terms searchers use to find the sites they want. Your task is to match the words people are searching for to the ones you have on your site. It's a fact that if you don't include the word 'dalek' on your site, people using the word 'dalek' to search won't find you, for instance. We looked in Chapter 5, 'Getting ready for a successful eBay sale', at research-ing your keywords for your selling descriptions, understanding which were the most popular and making sure you use them. The same principle applies here too.

Get to know your keywords by using the research tools avail-able, as discussed earlier, and make sure you have a site that is rich in content that includes these keywords. Obviously, the pages describing your goods will include lots of lovely keywords, but think about other options as well. A blog can easily be slot-ted into a site and it's a great way of making sure you're regularly adding more content (search engines reward recently and regularly updated sites); think too about writing articles on relevant topics and adding pages about you, your business and sales. It all adds up.

But not overdoing it!

If your content is good prose crafted as genuine copy for the ben-efit of your users, you'll never have a problem with search engines. However, some website owners try to game the system by disin-genuously cramming their sites full of relevant keywords. This could mean concealing long lists of words in their pages, repeat-ing keywords with unnatural frequency or simply building pages containing pointless text. This kind of practice isn't looked on kindly by Google. In fact, you sometimes hear about sites being delisted from Google altogether if they do this, which isn't good for attracting customers.

Getting linked in

The other things search engine sites love are links: links from your sites to other sites, links into your site from other websites, and also the links within your site that help the spiders navigate around and understand what the site is about. A key aspect of optimising your site is making sure you have as many links in and out of your site as possible. The number of links isn't the only aspect that matters: Google also takes into account what it considers to be the importance of the site the link is to.

> Tip: Link text
> Don't neglect the text of your links, as the spiders use the
> words to understand what the destination of the link is about.

Make sure you have an acceptable link from eBay to your site, maybe from your About Me page or shop as a first step. Then start building other links in from anywhere you can. In fact, this is an ongoing opportunity you should always have your eyes open for.

There are five main ways of building links:

> - **Link exchange**   Build a page on your site that's a list of links to other websites. Start with your friends and colleagues and offer to put a link in your list to their website in exchange for a link on their site. Soon you'll be able to build up a good long list and have lots of links into your site too.
> - **Comment on blogs**   Bloggers usually welcome comments and responses to their blog posts and when you post you're usually allowed to add a link to your own website that other readers can click on. It's well worth spending a few minutes now and again posting comments on blogs and getting more links coming in. This is also not a bad way of marketing in general: other people on the blog can see your link, follow it and maybe buy something, and it's also a way of telling people who you are. Choose popular, relevant blogs and comment on as wide a selection as possible.
> - **Build profiles**   There are squillions of sites that allow you to build a profile and tell the world about you and your business. Most of them are free and in the most part they only take a few moments to establish a presence on.
> - **Join communities and networks**   Twitter, YouTube, chat boards, discussion boards and any online community forum that permits you to make a contribution are opportunities to get a link into your site. But be careful you don't fall foul of any rules that ban advertising. Lots of sites don't let you blatantly plug your own site, but you can often find ways of doing

it legitimately – see what other people are doing and emulate their tactics. On some chat boards, for instance, you're not permitted to link to your site in posts, but you are allowed a personalised 'signature' that can include a website link.

> **Join directories** Don't forget to ensure your web address is included in as many online directories as possible. These come in all shapes and sizes. Some are the online versions of the phone book or Yellow Pages and you should certainly include your web address in these. Others are local or centred around a theme or interest area, such as parenting or angling. Start with Google and see what else exists that's relevant to you. Don't forget that links from classified sites count too, so seek out Gumtree, craigslist, LinkedIn and others and add your links where you're permitted to do so.

> Tip: Google toolbar

Download the Google toolbar to see how you're doing in search. This sits at the top of your browser wherever you are on the web. The toolbar includes a service called 'page rank', which is a speedy way of seeing how Google rates your site. The higher the page rank, the greater the importance of your site in Google's eyes. It also has lots of handy features, so it's well worth getting hold of. You can find it here:
> http://toolbar.google.co.uk

SEARCH ENGINE ADVERTISING >

An eBay seller once wistfully told me that advertising with Google was 'a good way to make a small fortune'. I was surprised and asked if he meant it. He said, 'Oh yes, out of a big one.' He wasn't joking.

The previous section examined how to optimise your website to ensure as much free traffic as possible comes your way from search engines. You don't pay the search engine a penny for 'natural search' traffic. Needless to say, it's also possible to buy advertising. By paying you can ensure your site is nearer to the top of the list and more visible to buyers. It can take weeks and months for your site even to show up and start performing naturally, but with advertising you can achieve an instant presence.

Google sells advertising space and people buy it – people buy it in droves, which is why Google's founders are billionaires. It's been said that of all the money spent worldwide on advertising, 1% is spent with the search giant.

If you've ever searched Google you'll have seen its adverts. They appear in two places in Google search results: at the top and on the right-hand side. Google is also greatly expanding where it displays paid-for ads. For instance, if you use Googlemail, you often see paid-for ads in your inbox, relevant to the emails you've been sending and receiving. Google also has map services that show ads on them.

But probably the most innovative and clever thing Google does to distribute its advertising is to allow people to display Google ads on their own sites. Any time someone clicks an ad a website owner is showing, the website owner gets paid. The programme is called Adsense and you can discover all about it at:

> www.google.co.uk/intl/en/ads

Paying per click

One of the reasons Google can feel expensive to people more used to the eBay model is that you don't pay per sale but rather per click. If someone clicks a link you're paying for, you have to cough up, regardless of whether that person goes on to buy something. This means it's possible to spend money and not get any additional sales, which grates. If your model is based around the price and sales per item, you might need to change your system.

One way of doing that might be setting up a marketing budget that can be used generally to promote your business and is kept separate from 'per item' spending. From that budget you can allocate some spending to Google Adwords. Even though you can't directly attribute the spend to sales, you can limit your

expenditure to the amount of the budget and prevent your costs spiralling out of control.

However, before you start thinking about spending money, make sure you've cracked natural search. Spending on advertising before your SEO is sorted is rather like opening a shop on the high street and only letting in people who've got an invitation, rather than opening the doors to allow passers-by to enter.

If you do decide to pay, setting up an account with Adwords is pretty easy and getting your ads on Google shouldn't take long. You create your own adverts with the information you want to present to searchers and then choose the keywords with which you want your ads to be associated. You agree what you're willing to spend and then Google displays the ad when it's relevant to a search result. The placement of your ad is determined by Google and by how appropriate it is to the search in question.

Setting up an account

Set up your Adwords account at:

> https://adwords.google.co.uk

You need to provide some personal details so that Google can keep in touch with you. Next, choose whether you want the starter version of the programme or the standard one. Go with the Starter Edition if you're completely new to Adwords; don't worry, you can upgrade whenever you want.

Creating your advert

Once you're set up, you need to build your advert. First, express a preference about who will see your ad. Will you make it visible to all international viewers or limit it to local searchers? For a business that's graduated from eBay, it's probably not sensible to limit your viewers to those who are local; that's an option better suited to businesses such as restaurants or services that make the majority of their trade from customers close by.

You then have to write the advert itself. There are three text fields you need to fill in to build your ad and you can see what it will look like as you go along. Think about the message you want to put across and craft a few tight lines of text that will attract clickers.

You're not limited to simply advertising your shop homepage. You have complete flexibility over what you promote: it could be a certain section of your website or even an individual product that you know sells well and will attract traffic.

Tip: Your budget

It's unlikely you'll have much success with a budget of less than £30 a month. However, you can set a budget as low or as high as you like and Google won't exceed that limit. Even £10 a week can help you understand your keywords and what's effective.

Choosing your keywords

When do you want your advert to show up? What words will someone be searching for to get your ad? You'll doubtless have lots of ideas about what you want, but Google can also provide you with ideas and suggestions based on what people have searched for in the past. Take a moment or two to validate your ideas and hone your keywords. Don't merely select your business name or a narrow interpretation; try to include relevant keywords that relate to your sales in a broader sense.

Pricing it up

The keywords you choose also determine the price you pay to Google for your clicks. But it's not as simple as keyword x costing y pence per click. The price is determined by an auction in which you compete with the other people who want to buy the same keywords. If you bid higher than other people, you'll more than likely get your ad to appear at the top of the sponsored link section.

So if you set your maximum bid for the word 'gramophone' at 35p and the nearest other bid is 24p, you'll get priority over other ads when people search for 'gramophone'. Google won't charge you 35p when someone clicks, it will charge you 25p, a penny more than the next highest bidder. Even if you're not the highest bidder, or even the second highest bidder, your ad will still show up; it just won't show up as often or as high up the list as people who are bidding more.

What's particularly smart about Adwords is that money's not the only deciding option. Google's integrity relies on the relevance of the results and ads it shows to searchers. Because relevance is key, low bidders can still enjoy visibility by being a popular ad that lots of people have clicked on in the past. This means a well-framed, successful advert can knock the socks off ads placed by bidders with more money.

Once you've determined the details, before you send your advert live you have to provide payment details so that Google can bill you.

Managing your campaign

You can manage your ad from a console on the Adwords website. You can see how the ad is performing, how many clicks you're getting, where those clicks are coming from, which keywords are working best and what you're spending. You can also make changes and corrections to ensure better performance here.

It might be tempting to search for your ad to make sure it's appearing and then click on the link to ensure that's working correctly, but try not to: you still have to pay for the clicks you make

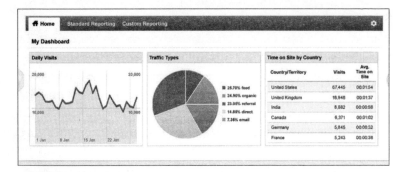

yourself. And if you want to manage multiple ads, you need to upgrade to the standard version of Adwords.

There's little doubt that Adwords is a potentially powerful way of advertising. Google is the biggest thing on the net, attracting millions of searchers a day, and you need to plug into that potent powerhouse to succeed. Nevertheless, Adwords can be a time-consuming and difficult beast to tame. Start slowly, learn the ropes, ramp up and keep at it. The rewards are potentially worth the effort.

MEASURING YOUR SITE'S PERFORMANCE>

Making the most of Google demands that you spend some time analysing your statistics and performance numbers. Google provides an amazing free tool to help you keep track of your website, called Google Analytics:

> www.google.com/analytics/en-GB

This can really help you understand who's visiting your site, where they're coming from and how they're finding you. A thorough understanding of these vital nuts and bolts can also help you better target your SEO efforts and become more efficient with your Adwords spending.

SEARCH ENGINE MARKETING CHECKLIST >

> **Optimise your website for search engines**   Help the spiders to catalogue and index your site by understanding and paying attention to SEO.
> **Build links and content**   Make your site as attractive as possible by developing lots of links in and out and producing keyword-rich content.
> **Experiment with Adwords**   Take the plunge and see what results you can get with Google Adwords.
> **Know the numbers**   Understand where your site traffic is coming from by exploring Google Analytics.

23 | Business essentials

> Every new or small business will have a series of forms it needs to fill in or things it needs to learn, but the requirements often change and can be bewildering. Don't worry – there's a host of help out there, you just have to know where to find it.

TAX AND VAT >

Her Majesty's Revenue and Customs has recently started targeting what it terms as 'etraders' with a new page:
> http://www.hmrc.gov.uk/guidance/selling/index.htm

HMRC is keen for online sellers to come forward and get registered, and has let it be known that it's also compiling information proactively. It has a special 'spider' that's crawling the web collecting details about sellers who look like they should be paying tax. The implication is that if you don't come forward voluntarily, you should expect a knock on the door.

The guidance from the HMRC website is pretty clear: 'If you sell the odd, unwanted gift or some personal possessions, you might not qualify as a trader. But if you buy items with the intention of selling them on as quickly and as profitably as you can, then you are a trader and likely to be self-employed.'

So if you've been buying in stock, you should get on the case and go legit.

> Inside Information: Registering as self-employed
You need to register as self-employed within three months of beginning to operate as such. If you don't, you might be liable to a penalty. So when you place that first order for goods you're going to sell on, it might be a good time to fill in the forms. You can do this online at:
> www.hmrc.gov.uk/startingup/register.htm

It's also essential to ensure you're making the Class 2 National Insurance contributions that are required from a self-employed person. You can pay these monthly or six-monthly by direct debit or when HMRC sends you a bill. You're also required to pay class 4 National Insurance and income tax on your profits, which is done through your self-assessment tax form each year.

Self-assessment is easily completed online as long as you're registered with the HMRC website. Make sure you have requested your password and activated your account well in advance of the deadlines to avoid a panic or a fine. You can register online at:

> www.hmrc.gov.uk/individuals/iwtfile-a-self-assessment-tax-returnonline.shtml.

When you're self-employed you're also liable to pay VAT if you exceed the threshold (a turnover of £77,000 at the time of writing), but unless you're turning over tens of thousands of pounds don't worry. I'd heartily advise getting professional input from an accountant or business expert even if you're not hitting the VAT limit. There's a lot to absorb as you set up a business and a mentor or guide will be invaluable and save you a great deal of needless fretting.

ASKING THE EXPERTS >

In addition to the tax authorities themselves, you'd be astonished by the huge amount of business advice and expertise that is available if you seek it out. Much of it is free and I've heard of some eBayers getting free accounting for two years, personalised mentoring and support funded by Europe, as well as ongoing business advice from experts. This shouldn't be surprising, because governments of every political persuasion love small businesses and want to see more of them succeeding.

If you've never run your own business before, all the paperwork and regulations can seem rather daunting. Should you be a sole trader, create a partnership, form a limited company, become VAT registered? The decisions you make depend on your individual circumstances and your aspirations; while you'll be able to get all sorts of advice, the decisions are ultimately up to you.

Check out the National Federation of Enterprise Agencies' website at www.nfea.com. This organisation specialises in information for small businesses and business start-ups. If you want to ask its advisers a specific question for free, it has a handy service at:

> www.smallbusinessadvice.org.uk/sbas.asp

The Institute of Business Advisers is another independent and respected organisation of individuals who can advise you on specific issues related to your business. You can find its website at:

> www.iba.org.uk

And think local too. There's doubtless a Chamber of Commerce down your way that will know all sorts of stuff that can help. You can find your nearest branch by looking on the national Chamber of Commerce website:

> http://www.britishchambers.org.uk/

Q & A WITH EMMA JONES >

Emma Jones MBE is one of Britain's leading authorities on business start-ups and small to medium enterprises. She's the brains behind the marvellous enterprisenation.com, a community for homegrown businesses that also works with the government on Start-Up Britain:

> www.startupbritain.co/

I asked her about some of the benefits of good admin and also where you can find extra help.

Q: What are the benefits of getting the paperwork in order?
A: The benefits are partly psychological in that you feel the business is more in order when the paperwork is intact, but there's also an aspect which is about complying with legal requirements.

When you start a business, it's good to open a business bank account so you can keep personal and business finances separate, to let the taxman (HM Revenue & Customs) know you are operating as a business.. This is straightforward to do and sets you up as a proper trading entity and makes customers feel more secure about buying from you. With the paperwork in order, you can focus on growing the business!

Q: Exactly what sort of things do you need to do to establish a new business?

A: On the legalities, you can register a limited company with a company formation agent such as Companies Made Simple. Within three hours, and for £16.99, you will have a certificate of proof that you are a company.

To start a business, I do advise having a business plan that serves as your route map – and it's good to have some customers too! Find them first through friends and family and then by promoting your wares via a blog, your own trading website and social media, as well as raising your profile through getting known in the press that covers your particular trade. With a product to sell and a list of hot contacts, you're well on your way to becoming your own boss.

Q: Lots of people are daunted by starting a business, should they be?

A: No! But what I do advise is you take things step by step so that starting a business doesn't seem so daunting. Start by 'working 5 to 9', which is the term I apply to the millions of people who are holding on to the day job and building a business at night and weekends. This way, you keep the security of a salary while building cashflow in the business and confidence in your own abilities. You'll surprise yourself how making a first sale, writing a press release or hosting a launch event doesn't seem daunting at all after you've achieved it.

Q: What help and resources are there for people starting a business?

A: Start-ups are the new rockstars and there's plenty of support available, from the government's StartUp Loans scheme for the under-30s, to memberships such as my own at Enterprise Nation, which connect businesses to each other for mutual and peer support. StartUp Britain is a campaign of which I'm a co-founder and through the campaign we have worked to point start-ups to the best resources as well as hosting Industry Weeks, StartUp Days, a national StartUp Tour (in a big bus that stays on the road for a month meeting thousands of potential entrepreneurs) and filling empty shops with small businesses through PopUp Britain.

There is support available for start-ups from the government, from large corporates who want to help, and from others travelling the same path. It's a much more supportive and collaborative environment than when I started my first business 13 years ago.

Q: Is now a good time to start a business?

A: It's a great time to start a business in Britain and the figures stand testimony to this. 2012 saw a record 484,000 companies formed and the ambition of StartUp Britain is to break the half a million record. With the entrepreneurial energy coming from people of all ages, sectors and backgrounds, this looks highly possible and will certainly be something to celebrate.

PARTNERSHIPS AND LIMITED COMPANIES >

If you're running a small enterprise and not employing anyone, it's perfectly possible to continue to operate as a sole trader as long as you want. However, your circumstances might warrant another approach. For instance, if there are two of you in the business you might want to create a formal deed of partnership. In a partnership each partner pays income tax as well as Class 2 and 4 National Insurance contributions like a sole trader.

You might also want to consider forming a limited company. You can buy an existing company via an agent or form one yourself via Companies House:

> www.companieshouse.gov.uk

Limited companies have to adhere to set legal requirements and must display company details on their premises and stationery. A limited company also has to file certain documents and the tax obligations are different from those applying to sole traders and partnerships. Forming a company is a step best taken with the guidance of a solicitor or accountant, who can advise you on what is best for you.

> Tip: eBay Business Centre
You can also find a good deal of information and help on running a business in eBay's Business Centre:
> http://pages.ebay.co.uk/businesscentre

BUSINESS PLANS AND ACCOUNTS >

The first kind of paperwork you need to turn your hand to is some sort of business plan. The scale of the plan will depend on what you're using it for. If it's to be presented to the bank manager for the purposes of getting finance, then it needs to be detailed enough to satisfy the bank's lending requirements. But if it's just for you to use in forecasting expenditure, sales and income, it won't have to be so robust.

At its most basic, your plan will detail the costs of setting up your business and keeping it going, forecast your sales and also project running costs. You want to spend some time thinking about a marketing plan and the future development of your business as well. You can find examples of different business plans online — there are some links here:

> https://www.gov.uk/write-business-plan

You can also get all sorts of guidance from the various bodies mentioned in this chapter. If you'll be presenting the plan to the bank, that organisation will also be able to give you information on what financiers require.

Above all, your plan must be realistic and achievable. There is no point in overforecasting your expected sales or profits. Make sure you factor in all your selling fees and the extras like postage and packaging material. As you grow you'll acquire greater expenses: maybe staff, premises, insurance, business rates and so on.

The other paperwork and records you need to keep are accounts. That means detailing the money you receive for your sales and what you spend. How you do that is up to you, but the best stop for information on what the tax man wants is the tax office itself. Your records can be as simple as an accounts book or you can keep a computer spreadsheet detailing your sales. What you want to avoid at the end of your first year is a shoebox full of receipts and only a vague notion of what you've actually sold. Keep good records from day one and that will save you loads of aggravation in the long run.

This could be a good opportunity to take a course in bookkeeping to make sure you're doing everything correctly, or perhaps invest in some accounting software to keep track of the numbers. Whatever you do, keep on top of the paperwork and don't leave it until the end of the year. In fact, part of your operations plan should include regular slots of time to update your records.

Many business sellers say that engaging an accountant from the outset is money well spent, but that's no substitute for keeping records as you go along. What you want to be able to do is present your accountant with sound records at the end of the year and then let them weave their tax-efficient magic. Of course, an accountant can also be a very good source of general business advice.

> Inside Information: Tax doesn't have to be taxing
It may seem like a crazy suggestion, but the best people to talk to about tax are the tax authorities themselves. This will seem

even more bonkers: they're also actually very nice. Whenever I say this people look at me in disbelief, but if you think about it, why wouldn't they be?

They want us to pay our taxes and however much we all don't want to, we know we have to. That's that. It's far easier for the authorities to be open and approachable and cooperative from the start and help people pay their taxes than for them to come chasing after us in the long run. As you're starting your eBay business, get yourself along to your local tax office and find out for yourself. There will be lots of handy information and resources there to help you get started.

While I'm at it, I'll debunk another myth: eBay hasn't given everyone's sales information to the tax authorities. It's been reported in the press that eBay has opened its books for HMRC's free perusal, but that isn't the case. Obviously eBay has legal responsibilities to the tax authorities, but the Revenue would need to apply for information on a case-by-case basis. Don't forget, though, that eBay is a very transparent environment and if anyone wants to take at a look at your sales and guess how much you're making, they could do it with a simple browse through your feedback.

LAWS FOR ONLINE SELLERS >

When you trade as a business you need to be aware of the laws that govern your type of operation. Some regulations are general and relevant to all types of sellers, but some are particular to online selling. The business resources mentioned earlier will be able to give you more information, but here are the basics:

> **Trade Descriptions Act 1968**   The Trade Descriptions Act is familiar to most people and it governs anything that is sold in the UK. In essence, you must not apply false information to anything you sell or supply, or offer to supply. As any successful seller will tell you, you won't last long if you mislead buyers

about an item you're selling, so complying with this law is just common sense.

> **Sales of Goods Act 1979**   This Act says that as a seller you must ensure the items you are selling are as you say they are, of a satisfactory quality and fit for their purposes. For any eBay seller, being open and honest in your description will be second nature already, so complying with this won't be a challenge if you're serious about making a success of your sales.

> **Consumer Protection (Distance Selling) Regulations 2000**   Commonly referred to as the Distance Selling Regulations or DSR, these apply to sales, such as on eBay, where no face-to-face contact occurs between the trading partners involved. If you're a business seller on eBay you have to make sure your buyers have a seven-working-day cooling-off period, during which they can cancel the contract. Under the DSR you must also provide information about yourself and the items you are selling.

> **Electronic Commerce (EC Directive) Regulations 2000**   This is another law that applies to online sales only. In addition to the requirements of the DSR, a business seller must detail their postal address and email address. If you belong to any trade organisation or an authorisation scheme relevant to your internet sales, you must also disclose the details. If as a seller you are VAT registered and your online sales are subject to VAT, you must publish your VAT number on eBay.

> ## Inside Information: The ecommerce law expert

Jane Bell is an eBay expert and she runs a business advising ecommerce traders on how to sell more. She's also a fount of knowledge on ecommerce law. I asked her for some golden advice and here are her wise words.

The law covering ecommerce purchases is different from high street retail shopping when it comes to returns and refunds. If you sell online it's imperative to get acquainted with the rights of your buyers. If you get it wrong you could end up in the courts and this has happened to a couple of famous retailers who didn't follow the EC Distance Selling Regulations.

When looking at marketplace traders, a fair percentage of these are small to medium enterprises: they started selling as a hobby and have grown into a fully fledged business. The most typical way of adding T&Cs to their online listings has been to copy that of another seller, perhaps one they see as more experienced. But this unfortunately can land you in court. Just because one of your peers has nicely written T&Cs doesn't mean they are correct in law and it's your responsibility to make sure your terms are correct, as it's you who will face the consequences if they are not.

When they're shopping online you have to give your buyers the confidence to buy. The law allows the purchase of an item and on receipt the buyer can examine it for size, fit, colour and quality. If it isn't suitable for any reason, then it can be returned for a full refund. There are some exclusions, so you should refer to the Office of Fair Trading website for details:

> http://www.oft.gov.uk/shared_oft/business_leaflets/ general/oft913.pdf

Let your buyers know their rights and it will give them confidence to buy from you.

The most typical mistakes usually concern accepting returns and refunds of postage and packing. Most instant purchases (and Second Chance offers on eBay) are covered by the EC Directive.

So in a nutshell, here are the three important points in relation to returns:

> Refund in full including the original postage charge and do not deduct any postage costs.
> The buyer should pay the cost to return the item, but only if you have told them this prior to the sale, unless it is a faulty or substitute item. Of course, you can offer free returns, where you refund the cost of returning the item to you as well.
> No restocking fees are allowed.

Visiting the Office of Fair Trading website is a great start to obtain its short and easy-to-understand, downloadable leaflets on the EC Directive covering distance selling:

> dshub.tradingstandards.gov.uk

I'd recommend you visit the site on a regular basis to keep up to date with changes in the legislation.

It's been a well-rehearsed refrain for a few years that small businesses can't get the credit they need to expand. Even profitable businesses with healthy profits and good prospects can find themselves surfing a fine line of positive cashflow. This can be a real issue that prevents growth and development, and in the worst cases it can be crippling. Keeping enough stock while ensuring suppliers are paid on time can seem like an impossible juggling act, so an unexpected expense can be the straw that breaks the camel's back.

ONLINE SOURCES >

It shouldn't be a surprise that one sector of business that has evolved a solution to this problem is ecommerce itself. Over the course of 2012, several companies emerged on the scene that aim to help online traders expand by providing finance. These new firms are typically small start-ups focused on supplying small businesses with money – and they aren't sharks.

Typically, these firms offer short-term loans at slightly higher than average (but hardly eye-watering) interest rates. Based on the ones I've met, they're run by clever guys with a background in finance who have really embraced the world of ecommerce. Not only do they carry out the same checks other credit companies might, they also take into account aspects such as your eBay feedback, trading data on eBay and Amazon and also social media activity to get a fuller picture of what your business is all about. It's hard to imagine a bank even knowing such things exist.

And what can the money be for? Two major areas that are vital for ecommerce sellers are good reasons to take out a loan such as this. The first is an investment in stock: if you haven't got it, you can't sell it. Taking a short-term loan to boost the coffers is a reasonable option if you spend on stock, thereby increasing revenues and driving profits. Indeed, if you can forecast a return on a loan relatively quickly and meet the payments, doing so makes sound business sense.

The second area would be capital investment in equipment and technology that will significantly improve the efficiency and effectiveness of your enterprise. It wouldn't take much of an uptick in productivity to justify a loan; indeed, if that means not taking on additional help, it's an even more obvious no-brainer.

Christoph Rieche is the CEO of one such company, called iwoca (short for instant working capital), and he explains how his business is already helping ecommerce sellers. 'We're seeing demand from all parts of the eBay trading community,' he says. 'We have customers who have well beyond £1m in revenue across eBay, Amazon and their own websites, down to customers who take in less than £50,000.

'We have built a model which assesses the risk of lending to an individual based on much more than just sales figures – the quality of customer feedback, how successful they are at attracting business through social media and credit history all go into the calculation. We ask for the same information the bank would, and then everything else we use is publicly available – the customer feedback and so on. A bank's system will not look at the eBay history, how active they are on social media. You need to be very online oriented, like us, to understand the benefit of these marketing strategies. We can assess a lot about them from that.'

Here are three companies that are worth checking out if you think a loan could help you. As ever, be sure to get a clear handle on the terms and proceed cautiously. Common sense goes a long way:

> **iwoca**   This is probably the market leader in the field and it is are based in London:
> > www.iwoca.co.uk
> **EZbob**   Offering loans of up to £40,000, EZbob promises a decision in half an hour:
> > www.ezbob.com

> **Kabbage**   Having cut its teeth in America, Kabbage is now looking to fund British ecommerce sellers:
> > https://uk.kabbage.com

> > Tip
> iwoca sponsors and organises regular meet-ups for online sellers to get together, hear some talks and have a chinwag over a beer. So far they've been held in London, Manchester, Birmingham and Bristol and are the only regular networking events for people selling on eBay and Amazon that I know of. I've been to a few – they're useful events and not at all a hard sell. Find out more at:
> > http://www.meetup.com/onlineselleruk/

CROWDFUNDING >

Many hands make light work could almost be an internet adage, and it's being applied online on behalf of charities and businesses in all sorts of ways. The trend for crowdfunding is one that's gathering momentum and numerous organisations on the web now allow you to pitch for a loan to their ready audience of lenders.

For a business wanting to secure a loan, this method gives you the chance to shine and make the case for why you need a cash injection to people who often have a good deal more imagination than the average bank manager.

There are several benefits for lenders. First, they can make a return on their capital that's better than they would obtain if they left it languishing in a savings account. The risk of the investment is also reduced because they aren't financing the whole loan, only a chunk alongside other crowd lenders.

There are a variety of services offering different levels of funding, with some catering for massive investments in start-ups and others concentrating on more modest loans for specific needs or projects. Nevertheless, what they seem to have in common is a typically benevolent approach and enlightened ethics. Needless to say, you'll be put through your paces to ascertain your credit-worthiness and the companies are regulated by the financial authorities. However, they do tend to be more dynamic and innovative than typical lenders.

Take your time to engage your instincts and experience when sizing up crowdfunding companies and judge whether it's the right path for you and your business.

Two well-regarded companies that I've encountered myself are:

> Crowdcube   www.crowdcube.com
> Funding Circle   www.fundingcircle.com

> Inside information: Borrow to grow
It goes without saying that one reason the world has got into the current economic mess is that cheap, plentiful credit was misused. It was employed to mask the real state of everything from household finances right up to the economies of nations. But even though credit was used badly, that doesn't mean credit is bad.

Cashflow is vital for a business and sometimes lacking access to a few thousand quid can have a detrimental effect. It can mean postponing investment in equipment or expertise. More annoyingly, it can mean you can't invest in stock when you know there's an opportunity to buy at a good price and there's demand aplenty from willing buyers.

In situations like that, if the sums all add up, you can take a loan, buy the goods, flog them, pay back the loan and interest quick smart and still turn a profit. That extra money you make can then be reinvested.

While it always pays to be cautious when borrowing, if the reason is to develop your enterprise, doing so could well make sense. Remember, though, it's not the right answer if you need a loan to plug a gap in the books because some part of your business is sick. Borrowing for that is merely perpetuating the problem and perhaps delaying the inevitable.

25 | Emerging trends in ecommerce

Wouldn't it be good to know the future? For a business, it would be a huge advantage to know how things in ecommerce will develop over the next five years or so. Sadly, that's impossible. But what is possible is to investigate the emerging trends that are visible now that might well help you think about your business and ensure it prospers in the years leading up to 2020.

This book has predominantly looked at getting started in ecommerce and then ramping up your business to a respectable level. Maintaining such an enterprise into the medium and longer term is a challenge that will require both guile and wits. It's not unachievable by any means (there are plenty of eBay sellers who've built multichannel businesses that are still going ten years after foundation), but as with any business the sands shift and you'll have to change too.

What is different with ecommerce, though, is the pace of change and to a great extent the sheer volume of it. When I cast my mind back to 1999 and think how far the internet has come since then, I can barely count the new and innovative things that have happened. Indeed, it all feels like a bit of a blur. It's not an understatement to say that the web has transformed business and commerce. There can be no more stark example of that than the music business: the great titans of the high street have crumbled in the face of the digital download. Books and publishing have also wobbled when confronted by Amazon, the Kindle and the multitudinous forces of self-publishing.

What is coming next?

YOUNG PRETENDERS >

The good news is that eBay and Amazon aren't going anywhere and they are likely to remain dominant in the market. Sometimes it may seem that they are killing their golden goose by squeezing sellers with fee increases and policy changes and alterations to the marketplace, but in time they'll have to learn to be more collegiate and concerned about maintaining good relationships with their merchants.

It's still astonishing to note that one reason ecommerce businesses fall by the wayside and die is because the big players like Amazon and eBay change something hastily and give sellers only a few weeks' notice. That cavalier attitude will inevitably shift – there isn't an infinite supply of entrepreneurs to keep selling.

The other reason these companies will have to treat their sellers better is that there is competition on the horizon and some of it is serious. New marketplaces are developing and they do seem, largely, to have a better handle on nurturing their sellers. These marketplaces don't look for the same breadth as eBay and Amazon; instead, they prefer to cultivate a niche and do it well. Etsy is a great example here: it's getting more and more traction, sellers and buyers wax lyrical about the service and it is truly a wonderful place to shop, expertly honed to the sellers and stock it's built for: craft sellers and artists.

The same goes for StubHub. eBay has always had a bit of bother with tickets and was often the butt of negative, critical press coverage when tickets were sold for sky-high prices well above their face value, so acquiring StubHub was a strategic move. We'll see more of that kind of development for sure – smaller, niche marketplaces doing less but so much better – and they won't all be bought out by the majors.

For at least a decade, Google has been touted as the great sleeping ecommerce giant, the king across the water who's most likely to be the killer of eBay or Amazon. However, I'm not sure that's true; or, indeed, entirely desirable. Aside from some minor dalliances with ecommerce in the form of Google Payments and Google Shopping (and whatever happened to the Froogle marketplace?), no innovation has emerged from Google that looks truly threatening to the status quo. In addition, Google has a reputation for being as thoughtless and faceless as the other corporations and it may even be more heavy-handed.

For those reasons, I think that the emergence of a handful of challenging, small players in ecommerce is a much more realistic and hopeful proposition.

BIG RETAILERS >

The first decade or so of the mass-market internet has been marked by many familiar high street names failing to fully understand ecommerce and integrate it into their businesses. For many, an ecommerce strategy was simply a matter of slapping a website up and hoping for the best, only to find that very little happened. What is even more astonishing is that some companies have shunned the emergence of ecommerce altogether, sniffed at it arrogantly and carried on as usual.

Some of these firms have paid the ultimate price. Electrical retail chain Comet died because it didn't 'get' ecommerce and didn't react as swiftly as its competitors. Supermarket Morrisons is having a tough time because it didn't offer online shopping to any real extent until 2013, making it very late to the party.

The bad news for ecommerce entrepreneurs, though, is that all these big players now know that ecommerce is essential and that they can't ignore it any longer. Indeed, the really clever ones have realised that it's by using their size and existing systems that they can gain greater control of ecommerce and offer specific services that consumers really like.

GETTING THE GOODS >

That leads to one intriguing realisation that's emerged in the past few years: people don't necessarily need to get the goods they buy online delivered directly to their door. Department store John Lewis and catalogue merchant Argos are two companies that have led the way here by pioneering what they call 'Click & Collect'. This has become so popular that you've probably done it yourself. You buy your items online and they're delivered to a store near you for you to collect. In John Lewis's case, Waitrose supermarkets are additional potential delivery hubs for people who might not live anywhere near a John Lewis branch.

The assumption that people don't need the goods delivered for the 'last mile' has also been picked up by two other delivery innovations. The first comes in the shape of the courier company Collect+, which doesn't deliver items to your door. Using a network of over 5000 local shops, your parcel is dropped at a local shop of your choosing (usual a corner shop open seven days a week and late into the evening) and you can pick it up from there at your convenience. This is obviously very attractive to those shoppers who aren't at home during the working week but don't fancy a time-consuming trek to a courier's local depot (which are often not that local).

The second has been pioneered by Amazon, which has started installing blocks of lockers in branches of the Co-op, tube stations and similar, beginning in London. On request, you have your orders sent to one of these lockers, which you open by punching a passcode into the computer on the front so you can retrieve your purchases.

Another delivery assumption that's being challenged is that the quickest you can get your goods that you've ordered online is the next day; as you will know, the delivery time can often be a lot longer than that. Both Amazon and eBay are experimenting with same-day delivery in some major metropolitan areas. In the UK, a company called Shutl is also pioneering delivery within hours. Services such as these do tend to attract a premium price, because a specific courier service is needed to make it happen, so they may not make it to the mainstream any time soon. Nevertheless, they're a useful reminder that ecommerce is getting faster and faster, and ecommerce entrepreneurs need to be aware that the pressure is on for them too.

MAKING IT MOBILE >

The biggest and greatest change to ecommerce reflects much bigger trends that are shaping the future of the internet itself. The web is no longer predominantly consumed by people at desks using computers. Indeed, desktops and laptops will soon seem as cutely archaic as cardboard punchcards and typewriters (with ribbons and Tippex). The smartphone revolution has happened very quickly and the majority of people in some countries now carry around a handset that has more power than their first full-size computer. Tablets, especially in the form of the seemingly ubiquitous iPad, have become the only interface some people use to access the World Wide Web.

This has dramatically changed how people shop and has awakened a whole new set of buyers who like the convenience of shopping on the move. 'Mobile shopping means people can use the "dead time" of their daily commute,' says Chris Dawson of Tamebay. 'eBay is seeing consumers using their smartphones in the morning on the way into the office, and again on the commute home. However, in the evening it is iPad and tablet use that shoots up, with the busiest time of day for tablets being between 5pm and 11pm at night.'

Where's all that going to lead? There are claims that the latest generation of smartphones will be able to be controlled by your eyes and simple gestures, and we'll doubtless see more of that sort of innovation. Wearable tech – like Google Glass, a computer in the form of high-tech spectacles controlled by voice commands – might also further develop the web and invigorate ecommerce.

It's difficult to predict where this might all lead us by 2020, but I guess we'll see soon enough. The message is to keep aware of technical and ecommerce trends and be imaginative about how they may apply to your own business.

That's all, folks

You may have found this book a bit of a roller-coaster ride. When you started reading it, you may never have sold anything online before. Now at the end, you've read all about founding, developing and running an ecommerce business selling across multiple channels, and you may well be well on the way to making that happen yourself.

One thing that will remain on the horizon for ecommerce is constant change. For my money that leads to two advantages. The first is that it keeps everything fresh and interesting. The need to review and monitor how everything is going means this kind of business is never dull. It also gives you a clear competitive advantage if you're the kind of businessperson who thrives on challenge.

The best way to stay in touch with me once you've read this book is via Tamebay.com, an eBay and ecommerce blog that I run with Chris Dawson. We're proud to be the number one blog for eBay and ecommerce small businesses in the UK and probably Europe too. Stop by and say hello.

You can also find my own blog at www.wilsondan.co.uk, where you can contact me direct. I tweet as @wilsondan and I'm on LinkedIn too, at uk.linkedin.com/in/danwilson.

Good luck!

Further reading

It pays all ecommerce entrepreneurs to keep up with the latest news and developments regarding eBay, Amazon, small business issues and the internet in general. Here are some ideas.

ChannelAdvisor has a triumvirate of blogs that I frequently turn to for views and comment:

> General company blog   http://blog.channeladvisor.com
> Scot Wingo's blog   http://ebaystrategies.blogs.com
> A blog about comparison
   shopping engines   http://www.csestrategies.com

You can find eBay's own official blog here:

> http://www.ebayinkblog.com

For hard news, check out the announcements on eBay's three biggest national sites, US, Germany and UK:

> www2.ebay.com/aw/marketing.shtml
> www2.ebay.com/aw/de-marktplatz.shtml
> www2.ebay.com/aw/marketing-uk.shtml

For a US perspective, take a look at Ecommercebytes (www.ecommercebytes.com), formerly known as Auctionbytes, a useful repository of knowledge and articles about eBay and other marketplaces as well as a blog.

Emma Jones (interviewed on page 218) is the brains behind Enterprise Nation and provides energetic and inspirational perspectives on small businesses and home-based enterprises:

> www.enterprisenation.com

I often turn to the various 'Donuts' for general business insights, ideas and tips. There are Donuts dedicated to law, IT, start-ups and tax, and the Marketing Donut is an invaluable resource:

> http://www.marketingdonut.co.uk/

The biggest organisation that looks across the full gamut of ecommerce is Internet Retailing and it has two useful resources I recommend. Its main site looks at retail and big business, but is a fascinating read:

> http://internetretailing.net/

Internet Retailing has also developed a blog and website for SMEs:

> http://esellermedia.com/

Learning Resources Centre
Middlesbrough College
Dock Street
Middlesbrough
TS2 1AD